THE DAILY STUDY BIBLE SERIES
REVISED EDITION

THE LETTERS TO THE
GALATIANS
AND
EPHESIANS

THE LETTERS TO THE
GALATIANS
AND
EPHESIANS

REVISED EDITION

Translated
with an Introduction and Interpretation
by
WILLIAM BARCLAY

THE WESTMINSTER PRESS
PHILADELPHIA

Revised Edition
Copyright © 1976 William Barclay

First published by The Saint Andrew Press
Edinburgh, Scotland

Galatians: First Edition, 1954; Second Edition, 1958
Ephesians: First Edition, 1956; Second Edition, 1958

Published by The Westminster Press ®
Philadelphia, Pennsylvania

PRINTED IN THE UNITED STATES OF AMERICA

4   5   6   7   8   9

Library of Congress Cataloging in Publication Data

Bible. N.T. Galatians. English. Barclay. 1976.
    The letters to the Galatians and Ephesians.

    (The Daily study Bible series — Rev. ed.)
    1. Bible. N.T. Galatians — Commentaries.
2. Bible. N.T. Ephesians — Commentaries. I. Barclay,
William, lecturer in the University of Glasgow.
II. Bible. N.T. Ephesians. English. Barclay. 1976.
III. Title. IV. Series.
BS2683.B37 1976   227'.4'077   76-22672
ISBN 0-664-21309-X
ISBN 0-664-24109-3 pbk.

GENERAL INTRODUCTION

The Daily Study Bible series has always had one aim—to convey the results of scholarship to the ordinary reader. A. S. Peake delighted in the saying that he was a "theological middleman", and I would be happy if the same could be said of me in regard to these volumes. And yet the primary aim of the series has never been academic. It could be summed up in the famous words of Richard of Chichester's prayer—to enable men and women "to know Jesus Christ more clearly, to love him more dearly, and to follow him more nearly".

It is all of twenty years since the first volume of *The Daily Study Bible* was published. The series was the brain-child of the late Rev. Andrew McCosh, M.A., S.T.M., the then Secretary and Manager of the Committee on Publications of the Church of Scotland, and of the late Rev. R. G. Macdonald, O.B.E., M.A., D.D., its Convener.

It is a great joy to me to know that all through the years *The Daily Study Bible* has been used at home and abroad, by minister, by missionary, by student and by layman, and that it has been translated into many different languages. Now, after so many printings, it has become necessary to renew the printer's type and the opportunity has been taken to restyle the books, to correct some errors in the text and to remove some references which have become outdated. At the same time, the Biblical quotations within the text have been changed to use the Revised Standard Version, but my own original translation of the New Testament passages has been retained at the beginning of each daily section.

There is one debt which I would be sadly lacking in courtesy if I did not acknowledge. The work of revision and correction has been done entirely by the Rev. James Martin, M.A., B.D., Minister of High Carntyne Church, Glasgow. Had it not been for him this task would never have been undertaken, and it is impossible for me to thank him enough for the selfless toil he has put into the revision of these books.

It is my prayer that God may continue to use *The Daily Study Bible* to enable men better to understand His word.

Glasgow   WILLIAM BARCLAY

CONTENTS

CONTENTS

CONTENTS

A GENERAL INTRODUCTION
TO THE LETTERS OF PAUL

THE LETTERS OF PAUL

There is no more interesting body of documents in the New Testament than the letters of Paul. That is because of all forms of literature a letter is most personal. Demetrius, one of the old Greek literary critics, once wrote, "Every one reveals his own soul in his letters. In every other form of composition it is possible to discern the writer's character, but in none so clearly as the epistolary." (Demetrius, *On Style*, 227.) It is just because he left us so many letters that we feel we know Paul so well. In them he opened his mind and heart to the folk he loved so much; and in them, to this day, we can see that great mind grappling with the problems of the early church and feel that great heart throbbing with love for men, even when they were misguided and mistaken.

THE DIFFICULTY OF LETTERS

At the same time there is often nothing so difficult to understand as a letter. Demetrius (*On Style*, 223) quotes a saying of Artemon, who edited the letters of Aristotle. Artemon said that a letter ought to be written in the same manner as a dialogue, because it was one of the two sides of a dialogue. In other words, to read a letter is like listening to one side of a telephone conversation. So when we read the letters of Paul we are often in a difficulty. We do not possess the letter which he was answering; we do not fully know the circumstances with which he was dealing; it is only from the letter itself that we can deduce the situation which prompted it. Before we can hope to understand fully any letter Paul wrote, we must try to reconstruct the situation which produced it.

THE ANCIENT LETTERS

It is a great pity that Paul's letters were ever called *epistles*. They are in the most literal sense *letters*. One of the great lights shed on the interpretation of the New Testament has been the discovery and the publication of the *papyri*. In the ancient world, *papyrus* was the substance on which most documents were written. It was composed of strips of the pith of a certain bulrush that grew on the banks of the Nile. These strips were laid one on top of the other to form a substance very like brown paper. The sands of the Egyptian desert were ideal for preservation, for papyrus, although very brittle, will last forever so long as moisture does not get at it. As a result, from the Egyptian rubbish heaps, archaeologists have rescued hundreds of documents, marriage contracts, legal agreements, government forms, and, most interesting of all, private letters. When we read these private letters we find that there was a pattern to which nearly all conformed; and we find that Paul's letters reproduce exactly that pattern. Here is one of these ancient letters. It is from a soldier, called Apion, to his father Epimachus. He is writing from Misenum to tell his father that he has arrived safely after a stormy passage.

" Apion sends heartiest greetings to his father and lord Epimachus. I pray above all that you are well and fit; and that things are going well with you and my sister and her daughter and my brother. I thank my Lord Serapis [his god] that he kept me safe when I was in peril on the sea. As soon as I got to Misenum I got my journey money from Caesar—three gold pieces. And things are going fine with me. So I beg you, my dear father, send me a line, first to let me know how you are, and then about my brothers, and thirdly, that I may kiss your hand, because you brought me up well, and because of that I hope, God willing, soon to be promoted. Give Capito my heartiest greetings, and my brothers and Serenilla and my friends. I sent you a little picture of myself painted by Euctemon. My military name is Antonius Maximus. I pray for your good health. Serenus sends good wishes, Agathos Daimon's boy, and Turbo, Gallonius's son." (G. Milligan, *Selections from the Greek Papyri*, 36.)

Little did Apion think that we would be reading his letter to his father 1800 years after he had written it. It shows how little human nature changes. The lad is hoping for promotion quickly. Who will Serenilla be but the girl he left behind him? He sends the ancient equivalent of a photograph to the folk at home. Now that letter falls into certain sections. (i) There is a greeting. (ii) There is a prayer for the health of the recipients. (iii) There is a thanksgiving to the gods. (iv) There are the special contents. (v) Finally, there are the special salutations and the personal greetings. Practically every one of Paul's letters shows exactly the same sections, as we now demonstrate.

(i) *The Greeting: Romans* 1: 1; 1 *Corinthians* 1: 1; 2 *Corinthians* 1: 1; *Galatians* 1: 1; *Ephesians* 1: 1; *Philippians* 1: 1; *Colossians* 2; 1 *Thessalonians* 1: 1; 2 *Thessalonians* 1: 1.

(ii) *The Prayer:* in every case Paul prays for the grace of God on the people to whom he writes: *Romans* 1: 7; 1 *Corinthians* 1: 3; 2 *Corinthians* 1: 2; *Galatians* 1: 3; *Ephesians* 1: 2; *Philippians* 1: 3; *Colossians* 1: 2; 1 *Thessalonians* 1: 1; 2 *Thessalonians* 1: 2.

(iii) *The Thanksgiving: Romans* 1: 8; 1 *Corinthians* 1: 4; 2 *Corinthians* 1: 3; *Ephesians* 1: 3; *Philippians* 1: 3; 1 *Thessalonians* 1: 3; 2 *Thessalonians* 1: 3.

(iv) *The Special Contents:* the main body of the letters.

(v) *Special Salutations and Personal Greetings: Romans* 16; 1 *Corinthians* 16: 19; 2 *Corinthians* 13: 13; *Philippians* 4: 21, 22; *Colossians* 4: 12–15; 1 *Thessalonians* 5: 26.

When Paul wrote letters, he wrote them on the pattern which everyone used. Deissmann says of them, "They differ from the messages of the homely papyrus leaves of Egypt, not as letters but only as the letters of Paul." When we read Paul's letters we are not reading things which were meant to be academic exercises and theological treatises, but human documents written by a friend to his friends.

THE IMMEDIATE SITUATION

With a very few exceptions, all Paul's letters were written to meet an immediate situation and not treatises which he sat down to write in the peace and silence of his study. There was some threatening situation in Corinth, or Galatia, or Philippi, or Thessalonica, and he wrote a letter to meet it. He was not in the least thinking of us when he wrote, but solely of the people to whom he was writing. Deissmann writes, "Paul had no thought of adding a few fresh compositions to the already extant Jewish epistles; still less of enriching the sacred literature of his nation. . . . He had no presentiment of the place his words would occupy in universal history; not so much that they would be in existence in the next generation, far less that one day people would look at them as Holy Scripture." We must always remember that a thing need not be transient because it was written to meet an immediate situation. All the great love songs of the world were written for one person, but they live on for the whole of mankind. It is just because Paul's letters were written to meet a threatening danger or a clamant need that they still throb with life. And it is because human need and the human situation do not change that God speaks to us through them today.

THE SPOKEN WORD

One other thing we must note about these letters. Paul did what most people did in his day. He did not normally pen his own letters but dictated them to a secretary, and then added his own authenticating signature. (We actually know the name of one of the people who did the writing for him. In *Romans* 16: 22 Tertius, the secretary, slips in his own greeting before the letter draws to an end.) In 1 *Corinthians* 16: 21 Paul says, "This is my own signature, my autograph, so that you can be sure this letter comes from me" (cp. *Colossians* 4: 18; 2 *Thessalonians* 3: 17).

This explains a great deal. Sometimes Paul is hard to understand, because his sentences begin and never finish; his grammar breaks down and the construction becomes involved. We must not think of him sitting quietly at a desk, carefully polishing each sentence as he writes. We must think of him striding up and down some little room, pouring out a torrent of words, while his secretary races to get them down.

When Paul composed his letters, he had in his mind's eye a vision of the folk to whom he was writing, and he was pouring out his heart to them in words that fell over each other in his eagerness to help.

THE LETTER TO THE GALATIANS

INTRODUCTION TO THE LETTER TO
THE GALATIANS

PAUL UNDER ATTACK

Someone has likened the letter to the Galatians to a sword flashing in a great swordsman's hand. Both Paul and his gospel were under attack. If that attack had succeeded, Christianity might have become just another Jewish sect, might have become a thing dependent upon circumcision and on keeping the law, instead of being a thing of grace. It is strange to think that, if Paul's opponents had had their way, the gospel might have been kept for Jews and we might never have had the chance to know the love of Christ.

PAUL'S APOSTLESHIP ATTACKED

It is impossible for a man to possess a vivid personality and a strong character like Paul and not encounter opposition; and equally impossible for a man to lead such a revolution in religious thought as he did and not be attacked. The first attack was on his apostleship. There were many to say that he was no apostle at all.

From their own point of view they were right. In *Acts* 1 : 21, 22 we have the basic definition of an apostle. Judas the traitor had committed suicide; it was necessary to fill the blank made in the apostolic band. They define the man to be chosen as one who must be "one of these men who were with us during all the time our Lord went in and out amongst us, beginning from the baptism of John, until the day he was taken from us" and "a witness of the Resurrection." To be an apostle a man must have companied with Jesus during his earthly life and have witnessed his Resurrection. That qualification Paul obviously did not fulfil. Further, not so very long ago he had been the arch-persecutor of the Christian Church.

In the very first verse of the letter Paul answers that. Proudly he insists that his apostleship is from no human source and that no human hand ordained him to that office, but that he received his call direct from God. Others might have the qualifications demanded when the first blank in the apostolic band was filled; but he had a unique qualification—he had met Christ face to face on the Damascus Road.

INDEPENDENCE AND AGREEMENT

Further, Paul insists that for his message he was dependent on no man. That is why in chapters 1 and 2 he carefully details his visits to Jerusalem. He is insisting that he is not preaching some second-hand message which he received from a man; he is preaching a message which he received direct from Christ. But Paul was no anarchist. He insisted that, although his message was received in entire independence, it yet had received the full approval of those who were the acknowledged leaders of the Christian Church (2: 6–10). The gospel he preached came direct from God to him; but it was a gospel in full agreement with the faith delivered to the Church.

But that gospel was under attack as well. It was a struggle which had to come and a battle which had to be fought. There were Jews who had accepted Christianity; *but* they believed that all God's promises and gifts were for Jews alone and that no Gentile could be admitted to these precious privileges. They therefore believed that Christianity was for Jews and Jews alone. If Christianity was God's greatest gift to men, that was all the more reason that none but Jews should be allowed to enjoy it. In a way that was inevitable. There was a type of Jew who arrogantly believed in the idea of the chosen people. He could say the most terrible things—"God loves only Israel of all the nations he has made." "God will judge Israel with one measure and the Gentiles with another." "The best of the snakes crush; the best of the

Gentiles kill." "God created the Gentiles to be fuel for the fires of Hell." This was the spirit which made the law lay it down that it was illegal to help a Gentile mother in her sorest hour, for that would only be to bring another Gentile into the world. When this type of Jew saw Paul bringing the gospel to the despised Gentile, he was appalled and infuriated.

THE LAW

There was a way out of this. If a Gentile wished to become a Christian, *let him become a Jew first*. What did that mean? It meant that he must be circumcised and take the whole burden of the law upon him. That, for Paul, was the opposite of all that Christianity meant. It meant that a man's salvation was dependent on his ability to keep the law and could be won by his own unaided efforts; whereas, to Paul salvation was entirely a thing of *grace*. He believed that no man could ever earn the favour of God. All he could do was accept the love God offered him by making an act of faith and flinging himself on his mercy. The Jew would go to God saying, "Look! Here is my circumcision. Here are my works. Give me the salvation I have earned." Paul would say:

> "Not the labours of my hands
> Can fulfil thy law's demands;
> Could my zeal no respite know,
> Could my tears for ever flow,
> All for sin could not atone:
> Thou must save, and thou alone.
>
> Nothing in my hand I bring,
> Simply to thy Cross I cling;
> Naked, come to thee for dress;
> Helpless, look to thee for grace;
> Foul, I to the fountain fly;
> Wash me, Saviour, or I die."

For him the essential thing was, not what a man could do for God, but what God had done for him.

"But," the Jews argued, "the greatest thing in our national life is the law. God gave that law to Moses and on it our very lives depend." Paul replied, "Wait one moment. Who is the founder of our nation? To whom were the greatest of God's promises given?" Of course, the answer is Abraham. "Now," went on Paul, "how was it that Abraham gained the favour of God? He could not have gained it by keeping the law because he lived four hundred and thirty years before the law was given to Moses. *He gained it by an act of faith.* When God told him to leave his people and go out, Abraham made a sublime act of faith and went, trusting everything to him. It was faith that saved Abraham, not law; and," Paul continues, "it is faith that must save every man, not deeds of the law. The real son of Abraham is not a man racially descended from him but one who, no matter his race, makes the same surrender of faith to God."

THE LAW AND GRACE

If all this be true, one very serious question arises—what then is the place of the law? It cannot be denied that it was given by God; does this emphasis on grace simply wipe it out?

The law has its own place in the scheme of things. First, it tells men what sin is. If there is no law, a man cannot break it and there can be no such thing as sin. Second, and most important, the law really drives a man to the grace of God. The trouble about the law is that because we are sinful men we can never keep it perfectly. Its effect, therefore, is to show a man his weakness and to drive him to a despair in which he sees that there is nothing left but to throw himself on the mercy and the love of God. The law convinces us of our own insufficiency and in the end compels us to admit that the only thing which can save us is the grace of God. In other words the law is an essential stage on the way to that grace.

In this epistle Paul's great theme is the glory of the grace of God and the necessity of realizing that we can never save ourselves.

GALATIANS

THE TRUMPET CALL OF THE GOSPEL

Galatians 1 : 1–5

> I, Paul, an apostle—and my apostleship was given to me from
> no human source and through no man's hand, because it came to
> me direct from Jesus Christ and from God the Father, who raised
> Jesus from the dead—with all the brothers who are here, write
> this letter to the Churches of Galatia. May grace and peace be on
> you from God the Father and from our Lord Jesus Christ, who,
> because our God and Father willed it so, gave his life for our
> sins, to rescue us from this present world with all its evil. Glory
> be to him for ever and ever. Amen.

To the people of Galatia there had come people saying that
Paul was not really an apostle and that they need not listen
to what he had to say. They based their belittlement on the
fact that he had not been one of the original twelve, that,
in fact, he had been the most savage of all persecutors of
the Church, and that he held, as it were, no official appoint-
ment from the leaders of the Church. Paul's answer was not
an argument; it was a statement. He owed his apostleship
to no man but to a day on the Damascus Road when he
had met Jesus Christ face to face. His office and his task
had been given him direct from God.

(i) Paul was certain that God had spoken to him. Leslie
Weatherhead tells of a boy who decided to become a minister.
He was asked when he had come to that decision and he
replied that it was after hearing a certain sermon in his school
chapel. He was asked the name of the preacher who had
wrought such an effect upon him. His answer was, "I do not
know the preacher's name; but I know that God spoke to
me that day."

In the last analysis no man can make another a minister
or a servant of God. Only God himself can do that. The real
test of a Christian is not whether or not he has gone through

certain ceremonies and taken certain vows; it is, has he seen Christ face to face? An old Jewish priest called Ebed-Tob said of the office which he held, "It was not my father or my mother who installed me in this place, but the arm of the Mighty King gave it to me."

(ii) The real reason for Paul's ability to toil and to suffer was that he was certain his task had been given him by God. He regarded every effort demanded from him as a God-given task.

It is not only men like Paul who have a task from God; to every man God gives his task. It may be one of which all men will know and which history will remember or it may be one of which no one will ever hear; but in either case it is a task for God. Tagore has a poem like this:

" At midnight the would-be ascetic announced:
    'This is the time to give up my home and seek for God. Ah,
      who has held me so long in delusion here?'
    God whispered, 'I,' but the ears of the man were stopped.
    With a baby asleep at her breast lay his wife, peacefully sleeping
      on one side of the bed.
    The man said, 'Who are ye that have fooled me so long?'
    The voice said again, 'They are God,' but he heard it not.
    The baby cried out in its dream, nestling close to its mother.
    God commanded, 'Stop, fool, leave not thy home,' but still he
      heard not.
    God sighed and complained, 'Why does my servant wander to
      seek me, forsaking me?' "

Many humble tasks are a divine apostolate. As Burns had it,

> To mak' a happy fire-side clime
>   For weans and wife,
> That's the true pathos and sublime
>   O' human life.

Paul's God-given task was to evangelize a world; to most of us it will simply be to make one or two folk happy in the little circle of those most dear.

Right at the beginning of his letter Paul sums up his

wishes and prayers for his friends in two tremendous words.

(i) He wishes them *grace*. There are two main ideas in this word. The first is that of *sheer beauty*. The Greek word *charis* means grace in the theological sense; but it always means beauty and charm; and even when theologically used the idea of charm is never far away from it. If the Christian life has grace in it, it must be a lovely thing. Far too often goodness exists without charm and charm without goodness. It is when goodness and charm unite that the work of grace is seen. The second idea is that of *undeserved generosity*, of a gift, which a man never deserved and could never earn, given to him in the generous love of God. When Paul prays for grace on his friends, it is as if he were saying, "May the beauty of the undeserved love of God be on you, so that it will make your life lovely, too."

(ii) He wishes them *peace*. Paul was a Jew, and the Jewish word *shalom* must have been in his mind, even as he wrote the Greek *eirene*. *Shalom* means far more than the mere absence of trouble. It means everything which is to a man's highest good, everything which will make his mind pure, his will resolute and his heart glad. It is that sense of the love and care of God, which, even if his body is tortured, can keep a man's heart serene.

Finally, Paul sums up in one sentence of infinite meaning the heart and the work of Jesus Christ. "He gave himself . . . to rescue us." (i) The love of Christ is a love *which gave and suffered*. (ii) The love of Christ is a love *which conquered and achieved*. In this life the tragedy of love is that it is so often frustrated; but the love of Christ is backed by an infinite power which nothing can frustrate and which can rescue its loved one from the bondage of sin.

THE SLAVE OF CHRIST

Galatians 1: 6–10

I am amazed that you have so quickly deserted him who called you by the grace of Christ, and that you have so soon gone over to a different gospel, a gospel which in point of fact is not another gospel at all. What has really happened is that certain men are upsetting your whole faith and are aiming at reversing the gospel of Christ. But even if we or an angel from heaven were to preach a gospel to you, other than that which you have received, let him be accursed. Is it men's favour I am trying to win, or is it God's? Or am I seeking to curry favour with men? If after all that has happened to me I were still trying to curry favour with men, I would not be bearing the brands of the slave of Christ.

THE basic fact behind this epistle is that Paul's gospel was a gospel of free grace. He believed with all his heart that nothing a man could do could ever earn the love of God; and that therefore all a man could do was fling himself on his mercy in an act of faith. All a man could do was take in wondering gratitude what God offered; the important thing was not what we could do for ourselves but what he had done for us.

It was this gospel of the free grace of God that Paul had preached. After him there came men preaching a Jewish version of Christianity. They declared that, if a man wished to please God, he must be circumcised and then dedicate his life to carrying out all the rules and regulations of the law. Every time a man performed a deed of the law, so they said, that was a credit entry in his account with God. They were teaching that it was necessary for a man to earn the favour of God. To Paul that was utterly impossible.

Paul's opponents declared that he was making religion far too easy and doing so to ingratiate himself with men. In fact that accusation was the reverse of the truth. After all, if religion consists in fulfilling a mass of rules and regulations, it is, at least theoretically, possible to satisfy its demands; but Paul is holding up the Cross and saying, "God loved you like that." Religion becomes a matter, not of satisfying the claims of *law*, but of trying to meet the obligation of *love*. A man can satisfy the claims of law, for they have strict and statutory limits; but he can never satisfy the claims of love, for if he gave his loved one the sun, the moon and the stars he still would be left feeling that that was an offering far too small. But all that Paul's Jewish opponents could see was that he had declared that circumcision was no longer necessary and the law no longer relevant.

Paul denied that he was trying to ingratiate himself with men. It was not men he was serving; it was God. It made no difference to him what men said or thought about him; his master was God. And then he brought forward an unanswerable argument. "If," he said, "I were trying to curry favour with men I would not be the slave of Christ." What is in his mind is this—the slave had his master's name and sign stamped on him with a red-hot branding iron; he himself bore on his body the marks of his sufferings, the brand of the slavery of Christ. "If," he said, "I were out to curry favour with men would I have these scars on my body?" The fact that he was marked as he was was the final proof that his aim was to serve Christ and not to please men.

John Gunther tells us of the very early communists in Russia. Many of them had been in prison under the Czarist regime and bore on their bodies the physical marks of what they had suffered; and he tells us that, so far from being ashamed of the marks which disfigured them, they were their greatest pride. We may be convinced that they were misguided and misguiding, but we can not doubt the genuineness of their allegiance to the communist cause.

It is when men see that we are prepared to suffer for the faith which we say we hold that they begin to believe that we really hold it. If our faith costs us nothing, men will value it at nothing.

THE ARRESTING HAND OF GOD

Galatians 1: 11–17

As for the gospel that has been preached by me, I want you to know, brothers, that it rests on no human foundation, for, neither did I receive it from any man, nor was I taught it, but it came to me through direct revelation from Jesus Christ. If you want proof of that—you heard of the kind of life I once lived when I practised the Jewish faith, a life in which I persecuted the Church of God beyond all bounds and devastated it. I was making strides in the Jewish faith beyond many of my contemporaries in my nation, for I was zealous to excess for the traditions of my fathers. It was then that God who had set me apart for a special task before I was born, and who called me through his grace, decided to reveal his Son through me, that I might tell the good news of him amongst the Gentiles. Thereupon I did not confer with any human being, nor did I go up to Jerusalem to see those who were apostles before I was; but I went away to Arabia; and then I went back again to Damascus.

IT was Paul's contention that the gospel he preached was no second-hand tale; it had come to him direct from God. That was a big claim to make and it demanded some kind of proof. For that proof Paul had the courage to point to himself and to the radical change in his own life.

(i) *He had been a fanatic for the law;* and now the dominant centre of his life was *grace.* This man, who had with passionate intensity tried to *earn* God's favour, was now content in humble faith to take what he lovingly offered. He had ceased to glory in what he could do for himself; and had begun to glory in what God had done for him.

(ii) *He had been the arch-persecutor of the Church.* He had "devastated" the Church. The word he uses is the word for utterly sacking a city. He had tried to make a scorched earth of the Church and now his one aim, for which he was prepared to spend himself even to death, was to spread that same Church over all the world.

Every effect must have an adequate cause. When a man is proceeding headlong in one direction and suddenly turns and proceeds headlong in the opposite direction; when he suddenly reverses all his values so that his life turns upside down; some explanation is required. For Paul the explanation was the direct intervention of God. He had laid his hand on his shoulder and arrested him in mid-career. "That," said Paul, "is the kind of effect which only God could produce." It is a notable thing about Paul that he is not afraid to recount the record of his own shame in order to show God's power.

He has two things to say about that intervention.

(i) It was no unpremeditated thing; it was in God's eternal plan. A. J. Gossip tells how Alexander Whyte preached the sermon when he was ordained to his first charge. Whyte's message was that all through time and eternity God had been preparing this man for this congregation and this congregation for this man and, prompt to the minute, he had brought them together.

God sends every man into the world with a part to play in his purpose. It may be a big part or it may be a small part. It may be to do something of which the whole world will know or something of which only a few will ever know. Epictetus (2: 16) says, "Have courage to look up to God and to say, 'Deal with me as thou wilt from now on. I am as one with thee; I am thine; I flinch from nothing so long as thou dost think that it is good. Lead me where thou wilt; put on me what raiment thou wilt. Wouldst thou have me hold office, or eschew it, stay or fly, be rich or poor? For all this I will defend thee before men.' " If a pagan philosopher could give himself so wholly to a God whom he knew so dimly, how much more should we!

(ii) Paul knew himself to be chosen for a task. He thought of himself as chosen not for honour but for service, not for ease but for battles. It is for the hardest campaigns that the general chooses his best soldiers and for the hardest studies that the teacher chooses his best students. Paul knew that he had been saved to serve.

THE WAY OF THE CHOSEN

Galatians 1: 18–25

Then, three years after that, I went up to Jerusalem to visit Cephas, and I stayed with him a fortnight. I saw no other apostle except James, the Lord's brother. As for what I am writing to you—

before God I am not lying. Then I went to the districts of Syria and Cilicia. But I remained personally unknown to the Churches of Judaea which are in Christ. The only thing they knew about me was that they were hearing the news—our one-time persecutor is preaching the faith which once he tried to devastate—and they found in me cause to glorify God.

WHEN we look at this passage alongside the last section of the preceding one we see just what Paul did when the hand of God arrested him.

(i) First, he went away to *Arabia*. He went away to be alone and for two reasons. First, he had to think out this tremendous thing that had happened to him. Second, he had to speak with God before he spoke to men.

There are so few who will take the time to face themselves and to face God; and how can a man meet the temptations, stresses and strains of life unless he has thought things out and thought them through?

(ii) Second, he went back to *Damascus*. That was a courage-ous thing to do. He had been on the way to Damascus to wipe out the Church when God arrested him and all Damascus knew that. He went back at once to bear his testimony to the people who knew best what he had been.

Kipling has a famous poem called *Mulholland's Vow*. Mulholland was a cattle-man on a ship. A storm broke out and in the storm the steers broke loose. Mulholland made a bargain with God that, if he saved him from the plunging horns and hooves, he would serve him from that time on. When he got safely to land he proposed to keep his part of the bargain; but his idea was to preach religion where no one knew him. Then came God's command, "Back you go to the cattle-boats and preach my gospel *there*." God sent him back to the place that he knew and that knew him. Our Christian witness, like our Christian charity, must begin at home.

(iii) Third, Paul went to *Jerusalem*. Again he took his life in his hands. His former friends, the Jews, would be out for his blood, because to them he was a renegade. His former victims, the Christians, might well ostracize him, unable to believe that he was a changed man.

Paul had the courage to face his past. We never really get away from our past by running away from it. We can deal with it only by facing it and defeating it.

(iv) Fourth, Paul went to *Syria and Cilicia*. It was there that Tarsus was. It was there that he had been brought up. There were the friends of his boyhood and his youth. Again he chose the hard way. They would no doubt regard him as quite mad; they would meet him with anger, and, worse, with mockery. But he was quite prepared to be regarded as a fool for the sake of Christ.

In these verses Paul was seeking to defend and prove the independence of his gospel. He got it from no man; he got it from God. He consulted no man; he consulted God. But as he wrote he unconsciously delineated himself as the man who had the courage to witness to his change and preach his gospel in the hardest places of all.

THE MAN WHO REFUSED TO BE OVERAWED

Galatians 2: 1–10

Fourteen years afterwards I again went up to Jerusalem with Barnabas, and I took Titus with me too. It was in consequence of a direct message from God that I went up; and I placed before them the gospel that I am accustomed to preach among the Gentiles, because I did not want to think that the work which I was trying to do, and which I had done, was going to be frustrated. This I did in private conference with those whose reputations stood high in the Church. But not even Titus, who was with me, was compelled to be circumcised, although he was a Greek. True they tried to circumcise him to please false brothers who had been furtively introduced into our society and who had insinuated themselves into our company to spy out the liberty which we enjoy in Christ Jesus, because they wished to reduce us to their own state of servitude. Not for one hour did we yield in submission to them. We took a stand that the truth of the gospel might remain with you.

Now from those who are men of reputation—what they once were makes no difference to me—there is no favouritism with God—those men of reputation imparted no fresh knowledge to me; but, on the other hand, when they saw that I had been entrusted with the preaching of the gospel in the non-Jewish world, just as Peter had been in the Jewish world—for he who worked for Peter, to make him the apostle of the Jewish world, worked for me too to make me the apostle to the non-Jewish world—and when they realized the grace that had been given to me, James, Cephas and John, whom all look upon as pillars of the Church, gave pledges of partnership to me and to Barnabas, in complete agreement that we should go to the non-Jewish world, and they to the Jewish world. The one thing which they did enjoin us to do was to remember the poor—the very thing that I myself was eager to do.

IN the preceding passage Paul has proved the independence of his gospel; here he is concerned to prove that this independence is not anarchy and that his gospel is not something schismatic and sectarian, but no other than the faith delivered to the Church.

After fourteen years' work he went up to Jerusalem, taking with him Titus, a young friend and henchman, who was a Greek. That visit was by no means easy. Even as he wrote there was agitation in Paul's mind. There is a disorder in the Greek which it is not possible fully to reproduce in English translation. Paul's problem was that he could not say too little or he might seem to be abandoning his principles; and he could not say too much, or it might seem that he was at open variance with the leaders of the Church. The result was that his sentences are broken and disjointed, reflecting his anxiety.

From the beginning the real leaders of the Church accepted his position; but there were others who were out to tame this fiery spirit. There were those, who, as we have seen, accepted Christianity but believed that God never gave any privilege to a man who was not a Jew; and that, therefore, before a man could become a Christian, he must be circumcised and take the whole law upon him. These Judaizers, as they are called, seized on Titus as a test case. There is a battle behind this passage; and it seems likely that the leaders of the Church urged Paul, for the sake of peace, to give in, in the case of Titus. But he stood like a rock. He knew that to yield would be to accept the slavery of the law and to turn his back on the freedom which is in Christ. In the end Paul's determination won the day. In principle it was accepted that his work lay in the non-Jewish world, and the work of Peter and James among the Jews. It is to be carefully noted that it is not a question of two different gospels being preached; it is a question of the same gospel being brought to two different spheres by different people specially qualified to do so.

From this picture certain characteristics of Paul emerge clearly.

(i) He was a man who gave authority its due respect. He did not go his own way. He went and talked with the leaders of the Church however much he might differ from them. It is a great and neglected law of life that however right we happen to be there is nothing to be gained by rudeness. There is never any reason why courtesy and determination should not go hand in hand.

(ii) He was a man who refused to be overawed. Repeatedly he mentions the reputation which the leaders and pillars of the Church enjoyed. He respected them and treated them with courtesy; but he remained inflexible. There is such a thing as respect; and there is such a thing as the grovelling, prudential bowing to those whom the world or the Church labels great. Paul was always certain that he was seeking the approval not of men but of God.

(iii) He was a man conscious of a special task. He was convinced that God had given him a task to do and he would let neither opposition from without nor discouragement from within stop him doing it. The man who knows he has a God-given task will always find that he has a God-given strength to carry it out.

THE ESSENTIAL UNITY

Galatians 2: 11–13

But when Peter came to Antioch, I opposed him to his face because he stood condemned. Before some men arrived from James it was his habit to eat with the Gentiles. When they came he withdrew and separated himself, because he was scared of the circumcision party. The rest of the Jews played the hypocrite along with him, so that even Barnabas was led away along with them by their hypocritical actions.

THE trouble was by no means at an end. Part of the life of the early Church was a common meal which they called the *Agape* or Love Feast. At this feast the whole congregation came together to enjoy a common meal provided by a pooling of whatever resources they had. For many of the slaves it must have been the only decent meal they had all week; and in a very special way it marked the togetherness of the Christians.

That seems, on the face of it, a lovely thing. But we must remember the rigid exclusiveness of the narrower Jew. He regarded his race as the Chosen People in such a way as involved the rejection of all others. "The Lord is merciful and gracious" (Psalm 2: 5). "But he is only gracious to Israelites; other nations he will terrify." "The nations are as stubble or straw which shall be burned, or as chaff scattered to the wind." "If a man repents God accepts him, but that applies only to Israel and no other nation." "Love all but hate the heretics." This exclusiveness entered into daily life. A strict Jew was forbidden even to do business with a Gentile; he must not go on a journey with a Gentile; he must neither give hospitality to, nor accept hospitality from, a Gentile.

Here in Antioch arose the tremendous problem, in face of all this could the Jews and the Gentiles sit down together at a common meal? If the old law was to be observed it was obviously impossible. Peter came to Antioch and, at first, disregarding the old taboos in the glory of the new faith, he shared the common meal with Jew and Gentile. Then came certain of the Jewish party from Jerusalem. They used James's name although quite certainly they were not representing his views, and they worked on Peter so much that he withdrew from the common meal. The other Jews withdrew with him and finally even Barnabas was involved in this secession. It was then that Paul spoke with all the intensity of which his passionate nature was capable, for he saw certain things quite clearly.

(i) A church ceases to be Christian if it contains class distinctions. In the presence of God a man is neither Jew nor Gentile, noble nor base, rich nor poor; he is a sinner for whom Christ died. If men share in a common sonship they must be brothers.

(ii) Paul saw that strenuous action was necessary to counteract a drift which had occurred. He did not wait; he struck. It made no difference to him that this drift was connected with the name and conduct of Peter. It was wrong and that was all that mattered to him. A famous name can never justify an infamous action. Paul's action gives us a vivid example of how one strong man by his steadfastness can check a drift away from the right course before it becomes a tidal wave.

THE END OF THE LAW

Galatians 2: 14–17

But when I saw that they were straying away from the right path which the gospel lays down, I said to Peter in front of them all, "If you who are a born Jew choose to live like a Gentile and not like a Jew, why are you forcing the Gentiles to live like Jews? We are by nature Jews; we are not Gentile sinners as you would call them; and we know that a man is not put right with God because he does the works which the law lays down, but through faith in Jesus Christ. Now we have accepted this faith in Jesus Christ, so that we might be right with God, and that faith has nothing to do with the works the law lays down, because no man can ever put himself right with God by doing the works the law lays down. Now if in our search to be made right with God through Christ Jesus we too become what you call sinners, are you then going to argue that Christ is the minister of sin? God forbid!"

HERE at last the real root of the matter is being reached. A decision is being forced which could not in any event be long delayed. The fact of the matter was that the Jerusalem decision was a compromise, and, like all compromises, it had in it the seeds of trouble. In effect the decision was that the Jews would go on living like Jews, observing circumcision and the law, but that the Gentiles were free from these observances. Clearly, things could not go on like that, because the inevitable result was to produce two grades of Christians and two quite distinct classes in the Church. Paul's argument ran like this. He, said to Peter, "You shared table with the Gentiles; you ate as they ate; therefore you approved in principle that there is one way for Jew and Gentile alike. How can you now reverse your decision and want the Gentiles to be circumcised and take the law upon them?" The thing did not make sense to Paul.

Now we must make sure of the meaning of a word. When the Jew used the word *sinners* of Gentiles he was not thinking of moral qualities; he was thinking of the observance of the law. To take an example—Leviticus 11 lays down which animals may and may not be used for food. A man who ate a hare or pork broke these laws and became a *sinner* in this sense of the term. So Peter would answer Paul, "But, if I eat with the Gentiles and eat the things they eat, I become a sinner."

Paul's answer was twofold. First, he said, "We agreed long ago that no amount of observance of the law can make a man right with God. That is a matter of grace. A man cannot earn, but must accept the generous offer of the love of God in Jesus. Therefore the whole business of law is irrelevant." Next he said, "You hold that to forget all this business about rules and regulations will make you a sinner. *But that is precisely what Jesus Christ told you to do.* He did not tell you to try to earn salvation by eating this animal and not eating that one. He told you to fling yourself without reserve on the grace of God. Are you going to argue, then, that he taught you to become a sinner?" Obviously there could be only one proper conclusion, namely that the old laws were wiped out.

This is the point that had to come. It could not be right for Gentiles to come to God by grace and Jews to come to him by law. For Paul there was only one reality, grace, and it was by way of surrender to that grace that all men must come.

There are two great temptations in the Christian life, and, in a certain sense, the better a man is the more liable he is to them. First, there is the temptation to try to earn God's favour, and second, the temptation to use some little achievement to compare oneself with our fellow men to our advantage and their disadvantage. But the Christianity which has enough of self left in it to think that by its own efforts it can please God and that by its own achievements it can show itself superior to other men is not true Christianity at all.

THE LIFE THAT IS CRUCIFIED AND RISEN

Galatians 2: 18–21

> If I build up again these very things that I destroyed, I simply succeed in making myself a transgressor. For through the law I died to the law that I might live to God. I have been crucified with Christ. True, I am alive; but it is no longer I who live but Christ who lives in me. The life that I am now living, although it is still in the flesh, is a life which is lived in faith in the Son of God, who loved me and gave himself for me. I am not going to cancel out the grace of God; for if I can get right with God by means of the law, then Christ died quite unnecessarily.

PAUL speaks out of the depths of personal experience. For him to re-erect the whole fabric of the law would have been spiritual suicide. He says that through the law he died to the law that he might live to God. What he means is this—he had tried the way of law; he had tried with all the terrible intensity of his hot heart to put himself right with God by a life that sought to obey every single item of that law. He had found that such an attempt produced nothing but a deeper and deeper sense that all he could do could never put him right with God. All the law had done was to show him his own helplessness. Whereupon he had quite suddenly abandoned that way and had cast himself, sinner as he was, on the mercy of God. It was the law which had driven him to God. To go back to the law would simply have entangled him all over again in the sense of estrangement from God. So great was the change that the only way he could describe it was to say that he had been crucified with Christ so that the man he used to be was dead and the living power within him now was Christ himself.

"If I can put myself to rights with God by meticulously obeying the law then what is the need of grace? If I can win my own salvation then why had Christ to die?" Paul was quite sure of one thing—that Jesus Christ had done for him what he could never have done for himself. The one man who re-enacted the experience of Paul was Martin Luther. Luther was a showpiece of discipline and penance, self-denial and self-torture. "If ever," he said, "a man could be saved by monkery that man was I." He had gone to Rome; it was considered to be an act of great merit to climb the Scala Sancta, the great sacred stairway, on hands and knees. He toiled upwards seeking that merit and suddenly there came to him the voice from heaven, "The just shall live by faith." The life at peace with God was not to be attained by this futile, never-ending, ever-defeated effort; it could be had only by casting himself on the love and mercy of God as Jesus Christ revealed them to men.

> "Pining souls! come nearer Jesus,
>   And O come, not doubting thus,
>   But with faith that trusts more bravely
>   His huge tenderness for us."

  If our love were but more simple,
   We should take him at his word;
  And our lives would be all sunshine,
   In the sweetness of our Lord."

When Paul took God at his word, the midnight of law's frustration became the sunshine of grace.

THE GIFT OF GRACE

Galatians 3: 1-9

O senseless Galatians, who has put the evil eye on you—you before whose very eyes Jesus Christ was placarded upon his Cross? Tell me this one thing—did you receive the Spirit by doing the works the law lays down, or because you listened and believed? Are you so senseless? After beginning your experience of God in the Spirit, are you now going to try to complete it by making it dependent upon what human nature can do? Is the tremendous experience you had all for nothing—if indeed you are going to let it go for nothing? Did he who generously gave you the Spirit, and who wrought mighty things among you, do so because you produced the deeds the law lays down or because you heard and believed? Was it not with you exactly as it was with Abraham—Abraham trusted God, and it was that which was credited to him as righteousness. So you must realize that it is those who make the venture of faith who are the sons of Abraham. Scripture foresaw that it would be by faith that God would bring the Gentiles into a right relationship with himself, and told the good news to Abraham before it happened—In you shall all nations be blessed. So, then, it is those who make that same venture of faith who are blessed along with Abraham, the man of faith.

PAUL uses still another argument to show that it is faith and not works of the law which puts a man right with God. In the early Church converts nearly always received the Holy Spirit in a visible way. The early chapters of *Acts* show that happening again and again (cp. *Acts* 8: 14–17; 10: 44). There came to them a new surge of life and power that anyone could see. That experience had happened to the Galatians and had happened, said Paul, not because they had obeyed the regulations of the law, because at that time they had never heard of the law, but because they had heard the good news of the love of God and had responded to it in an act of perfect trust.

The easiest way to grasp an idea is to see it embodied in a person. In a sense, every great word must become flesh. So Paul pointed the Galatians to a man who embodied faith, Abraham. He was the man to whom God had made the great promise that in him all families of the earth would be blessed (*Genesis* 12: 3). He was the man whom God had specially chosen as the man who pleased him. Wherein did Abraham specially please God? It was not by doing the works of the law, because at that time the law did not exist; it was by taking God at his word in a great act of faith.

Now the promise of blessedness was made to the descendants of Abraham. On that the Jew relied; he held that simple physical descent from Abraham set him on a different footing with God from other men. Paul declares that to be a true descendant of Abraham is not a matter of flesh and blood; the real descendant is the man who makes the same venture of faith. Therefore, it is not those who seek merit through the law who inherit the promise made to Abraham; but those of every nation who repeat his act of faith in God. It was by an act of faith that the Galatians had begun. Surely they are not going to slip back into legalism—and lose their inheritance.

This passage is full of Greek words with a history, words which carried an atmosphere and a story with them. In verse 1 Paul speaks about *the evil eye*. The Greeks had a great fear of a spell cast by the evil eye. Time and again private letters end with some such sentence as this: "Above all I pray that you may be in health *unharmed by the evil eye* and faring prosperously" (Milligan, *Selections from the Greek Papyri,* No. 14).

In the same verse he talks about Jesus Christ being *placarded* before them upon his Cross. It is the Greek word (*prographein*) that would be used for putting up a poster. It is actually used for a notice put up by a father to say that he will no longer be responsible for his son's debts; it is also used for putting up the announcement of an auction sale.

In verse 4 Paul talks about *beginning* their experience in the Spirit and *ending* it in the flesh. The words he uses are the normal Greek words for beginning and completing a sacrifice. The first one (*enarchesthai*) is the word for scattering the grains of barley on and around the victim which was the first act of a sacrifice; and the second one (*epiteleisthai*) is the word used for fully completing the ritual of any sacrifice. By using these two words Paul shows that he looks on the Christian life as a sacrifice to God.

In verse 5 he speaks of God giving generously to the Galatians. The root of this word is the Greek *choregia*. In the ancient days in Greece at the great festivals the great dramatists like Euripides and Sophocles presented their plays; Greek plays all have a chorus; to equip and train a chorus was expensive, and public-spirited Greeks generously offered to defray the entire expenses of the chorus. (That gift is described by the word *choregia*.) Later, in war time, patriotic citizens gave free contributions to the state and *choregia* was used for this, too. In still later Greek, in the papyri, the word is common in marriage contracts and describes the support that a husband, out of his love, undertakes to give his wife. *Choregia* underlines the generosity of God, a generosity which is born of love, of which the love of a citizen for his city and of a man for his wife are dim suggestions.

THE CURSE OF THE LAW

Galatians 3: 10–14

All who depend on the deeds which the law lays down are under a curse, for it stands written, "Cursed is everyone who does not consistently obey and perform all the things written in the book of the law." It is clear that no one ever gets into a right relationship

with God by means of this legalism, because, as the Bible says,
"It is the man who is right with God through faith who will live."
But the law is not based on faith. And yet the scripture says,
"The man who does these things will have to live by them." Christ
ransomed us from the curse of the law by becoming accursed for
us—for it stands written, "Cursed is every man who is hanged on
a tree." And this all happened so that in Christ Abraham's blessing
should come to the Gentiles, and so that we might receive the
promised Spirit by means of faith.

PAUL'S argument seeks to drive his opponents into a corner
from which there is no escape. "Suppose," he says, "you decide
that you are going to try to win God's approval by accepting
and obeying the law, what is the inevitable consequence?"
First of all, the man who does that has to stand or fall by his
decision; if he chooses the law he has got to live by it.
Second, no man ever has succeeded and no man ever will
succeed in always keeping the law. Third, if that being so,
you are accursed, because scripture itself says (*Deuteronomy*
27: 26) that the man who does not keep the whole law is under
a curse. Therefore, the inevitable end of trying to get right
with God by making the law the principle of life is a curse.

But scripture has another saying, "It is the man who is right
with God by faith who will really live" (*Habakkuk* 2: 4).
The only way to get into a right relationship with God, and
therefore the only way to peace, is the way of faith. But
the principle of law and the principle of faith are antithetic;
you cannot direct your life by both at one and the same
time; you must choose; and the only logical choice is to
abandon the way of legalism and to venture upon the way of
faith, of taking God at his word and of trusting in his love.

How can we know that this is so? The final guarantor
of its truth is Jesus Christ; and to bring this truth to us he
had to die upon a Cross. Now, scripture says that every man
who is hanged on a tree is accursed (*Deuteronomy* 21: 23);
and so to free us of the curse of the law, Jesus himself
had to become accursed.

Even at his most involved, and here he is involved, one

simple yet tremendous fact is never far from the mind and
heart of Paul—*the cost of the Christian gospel.* He could
never forget that the peace, the liberty, the right relationship
with God that we possess, cost the life and death of Jesus
Christ, for how could men ever have known what God was like
unless Jesus Christ had died to tell them of his great love.

THE COVENANT THAT CANNOT BE ALTERED

Galatians 3: 15–18

> Brothers, I can use only a human analogy. Here is the parallel—
> when a covenant is duly ratified, even if it is only a man's
> covenant, no one annuls it or adds additional clauses to it. Now
> the promises were made to Abraham and to his *seed.* It does not
> say, "and to his *seeds*," as if it were a case of *many,* but, "and to
> his *seed*," as if it were a case of *one,* and that one is Christ.
> This is what I mean, the law which came into being four hundred
> and thirty years later cannot annul the covenant already ratified
> by God and thus render the promise inoperative. For, if the
> inheritance is dependent on law, it is no longer dependent on
> promise; but it was through promise that God conferred his grace
> on Abraham.

WHEN we read passages like this and the next one, we have
to remember that Paul was a trained Rabbi, an expert in the
scholastic methods of the Rabbinic academies. He could,
and did, use their methods of argument, which would be
completely cogent to a Jew, however difficult it may be for
us to understand them.

His aim is to show the superiority of the way of grace over
the way of law. He begins by showing that the way of grace
is older than the way of law. When Abraham made his venture
of faith, God made his great promise to him. That is to say,
God's promise was consequent upon an act of faith; the law
did not come until the time of Moses, four hundred and
thirty years later. But—Paul goes on to argue—once a
covenant has been duly ratified, you cannot alter it nor add

additional clauses to it. Therefore, the later law cannot alter the earlier way of faith. It was faith which set Abraham right with God; and faith is still the only way for a man to get himself right with God.

The Rabbis were very fond of using arguments which depended on the interpretation of single words; they would erect a whole theology on one word. Paul takes one word in the Abraham story and erects an argument upon it. As the Authorized Version translates *Genesis* 17: 7, 8, God says to Abraham, "I will establish my covenant between me and thee and thy *seed* after thee" and says of his inheritance, "I will give it unto thee and to thy *seed* after thee." (*Seed* is more clearly rendered *descendant*, as the Revised Standard Version has it.) Paul's argument is that *seed* is used in the *singular* and not in the *plural;* and that, therefore, God's promise points not to a great crowd of people but to *one single individual;* and—argues Paul—the one person in whom the covenant finds its consummation is Jesus Christ. Therefore, the way to peace with God is the way of faith which Abraham took; and we must repeat that way by looking to Jesus Christ in faith.

Again and again Paul comes back to the same point. The problem of human life is to get into a right relationship with God. So long as we are afraid of him, there can be no peace. How are we to achieve this right relationship? Shall it be by a meticulous and even self-torturing obedience to the law, by performing endless deeds and observing every smallest regulation the law lays down? If we take that way we will be forever in default, for man's imperfection can never fully satisfy God's perfection; but if we abandon this hopeless struggle and bring ourselves and our sin to God, his grace opens its arms to us and we find ourselves at peace with a God who is no longer judge but father. Paul's argument is that this is what happened to Abraham. It was on that basis that God's covenant with Abraham was made; and nothing that came in later can change that covenant any more than anything can alter a will that has already been ratified and signed.

SHUT UP UNDER SIN

Galatians 3: 19–22

> Why, then, have the law at all? The law was added to the
> situation to define what transgressions are, until the seed should
> come, to whom the promise, which still holds good, had been
> made. That law was enacted by angels and came by means of a
> mediator. Now there can be no such thing as a mediator of one;
> and God is one. Is, then, the law contrary to the promises of
> God? God forbid! If a law which was able to give life had
> been given, then indeed right relationship with God would have
> come through the law. But the words of scripture shut up everything
> under the power of sin, for the very reason that the promise should
> be given to those who believe through faith in Jesus Christ.

THIS is one of the most difficult passages Paul ever wrote,
so difficult that there are almost three hundred different
interpretations of it! Let us begin by remembering that Paul
is still seeking to demonstrate the superiority of the way of
grace and faith over the way of law. He makes four points
about the law.

(i) Why introduce the law at all? It was introduced, as
Paul puts it, *for the sake of transgressions*. What he means
is that where there is no law there is no sin. A man cannot
be condemned for doing wrong if he did not know that it
was wrong. Therefore the function of the law is *to define sin*.
But, while the law can and does define sin, it can do nothing
whatever to cure it. It is like a doctor who is an expert in
diagnosis but who is helpless to clear up the trouble which he
has diagnosed.

(ii) The law was not given direct by God. In the old story in
Exodus 20 it *was* given direct to Moses; but in the days of
Paul the Rabbis were so impressed by the holiness and the
remoteness of God that they believed that it was quite impossible for him to deal direct with men; therefore they introduced the idea that the law was given first to angels and then
by the angels to Moses (cp. *Acts* 7: 53; *Hebrews* 2: 2). Here
Paul is using the Rabbinic thoughts of his time. The law is at a

double remove from God, given first to angels, and then to a mediator; and the mediator is Moses. Compared with the *promise*, which was given directly by God, the *law* is a second-hand thing.

(iii) Now we come to that extraordinarily difficult sentence—"There can be no such thing as a mediator of one; and God is one." What is Paul's thought here? An agreement founded on law always involves *two* people, the person who gives it and the person who accepts it; and it depends on both sides keeping it. That was the position of those who put their trust in the law. Break the law and the whole agreement was undone. But a promise depends on only *one* person. The way of grace depends entirely on God; it is his promise. Man can do nothing to alter that. He may sin, but the love and the grace of God stand unchanged. To Paul it was the weakness of the law that it depended on *two* persons, the law-giver and the law-keeper; and man had wrecked it. Grace is entirely of God; man can not undo it; and surely it is better to depend on the grace of the unchanging God than on the hopeless efforts of helpless men.

(iv) Is, then, the law antithetic to grace? Logically Paul should answer, "Yes" but, in fact, he answers, "No." He says that scripture has shut up everyone under sin. He is thinking of *Deuteronomy* 27: 26 where it is said that everyone who does not conform to the words of the law is cursed. In fact, that means *everyone*, because no one ever has, or ever will, perfectly keep the law. What, then, is the consequence of the law? It is to drive everyone to seek grace, because it has proved man's helplessness. This is a thought that Paul will soon develop in the next chapter; here he only suggests it. Let a man try to get into a right relationship with God via the law. He will find he cannot do it and will be driven to see that all he can do is to accept the wonderful grace of which Jesus Christ came to tell men.

THE COMING OF FAITH

Galatians 3: 23-29

> Before faith came we were under guard under the power of the law, shut up and waiting for the day when faith would be revealed. So that the law was really our tutor to bring us to Christ so that we might get into a right relationship with God by means of faith. But now that faith has come we are no longer under a tutor; for you are all sons of God through faith in Christ Jesus. As many of you as have been baptized into Christ have put on Christ. There is no longer any distinction between Jew and Greek, slave and free man, male and female, for you are all one in Christ Jesus. And if you belong to Christ, then you are the seed of Abraham, and heirs according to promise.

PAUL is still thinking of the essential part that the law did play in the plan of God. In the Greek world there was a household servant called the *paidagogos*. He was not the schoolmaster. He was usually an old and trusted slave who had been long in the family and whose character was high. He was in charge of the child's moral welfare and it was his duty to see that he acquired the qualities essential to true manhood. He had one particular duty; every day he had to take the child to and from school. He had nothing to do with the actual teaching of the child, but it was his duty to take him in safety to the school and deliver him to the teacher. That—said Paul—was like the function of the law. It was there to lead a man to Christ. It could not take him into Christ's presence, but it could take him into a position where he himself might enter. It was the function of the law to bring a man to Christ by showing him that by himself he was utterly unable to keep it. But once a man had come to Christ he no longer needed the law, for now he was dependent not on law but on grace.

"As many of you," says Paul, "who have been baptized into Christ have put on Christ." There are two vivid pictures here. Baptism was a Jewish rite. If a man wished to accept the Jewish faith he had to do three things. He had to be circumcised, to offer sacrifice and to be baptized. Ceremonial washing to cleanse from defilement was very common in Jewish practice (cp. *Leviticus*, chapters 11 to 15).

The details of Jewish baptism were as follows:—The man to be baptized cut his hair and his nails; he undressed completely; the baptismal bath had to contain 40 seahs, that is 2 hogsheads, of water. Every part of the body had to be touched with the water. He made confession of his faith before three men who were called *fathers of baptism*. While still in the water, parts of the law were read to him, words of encouragement were addressed to him, and benedictions were pronounced upon him. When he emerged he was a member of the Jewish faith; it was through baptism that he entered into that faith.

By Christian baptism a man entered into Christ. The early Christians looked on baptism as something which produced a real union with Christ. Of course, in a missionary situation where men were coming direct from heathenism, baptism was for the most part adult baptism and the adult would necessarily have an experience a child could not have. But just as really as the Jewish convert was united with the Jewish faith, the Christian convert was united with Christ (cp. *Romans* 6: 3ff.; *Colossians* 2: 12). Baptism was no mere outward form; it was a real union with Christ.

Paul goes on to say that they had put on Christ. There may be here a reference to a custom which certainly existed later. The candidate for baptism was clothed in pure white robes, symbolic of the new life into which he entered. Just as the initiate put on his new white robe, his life was clothed with Christ.

The result is that in the Church there was no difference between any of the members; they had all become sons of God. In verse 28 Paul says that the distinction between Jew and Greek, slave and free man, male and female is wiped out. There is something of very great interest here. In the Jewish morning prayer, which Paul must all his pre-Christian life have used, the Jew thanks God that "Thou hast not made me a Gentile, a slave or a woman." Paul takes that prayer and reverses it. The old distinctions were gone; all were one in Christ.

We have already seen (verse 16) that Paul interprets the promises made to Abraham as specially finding their fulfilment in Christ; and, if we are one with Christ, we, too, inherit the promises—and this great privilege comes not by a legalistic keeping of the law, but by an act of faith in the free grace of God.

Only one thing can wipe out the ever sharpening distinctions and separations between man and man; when all are debtors to God's grace and all are in Christ, only then will all be one. It is not the force of man but the love of God which alone can unite a disunited world.

THE DAYS OF CHILDHOOD

Galatians 4: 1–7

> This is what I mean—so long as the heir is an infant there is no difference between him and a slave, although he is owner of everything, but he is under the control of stewards and overseers until the day which his father has fixed arrives. It is just the same with us. When we were infants we were in subjection to the elementary knowledge which this world can supply. But when the fulness of time came, God sent forth his Son, born of a woman, born under the law, in order that he might redeem those who were subject to the law, so that we might be adopted as sons. Because you are sons, God sent forth the Spirit of his Son into our hearts, crying "Abba! Father!" The consequence is that you are no longer a slave but a son; and if a son, an heir because God made you so.

IN the ancient world the process of growing up was much more definite than it is with us.

(i) In the Jewish world, on the first Sabbath after a boy had passed his twelfth birthday, his father took him to the Synagogue, where he became *A Son of the Law*. The father thereupon uttered a benediction, "Blessed be thou, O God, who has taken from me the responsibility for this boy." The boy prayed a prayer in which he said, "O my God and God of my fathers! On this solemn and sacred day, which marks my passage from boyhood to manhood, I humbly raise my eyes unto thee, and declare with sincerity and truth, that henceforth I will keep thy commandments, and undertake and bear the responsibility of mine actions towards thee." There was a clear dividing line in the boy's life; almost overnight he became a man.

(ii) In Greece a boy was under his father's care from seven until he was eighteen. He then became what was called an *ephebos*, which may be translated *cadet*, and for two years he was under the direction of the state. The Athenians were divided into ten *phratriai,* or *clans*. Before a lad became an *ephebos*, at a festival called the *Apatouria*, he was received into the clan; and at a ceremonial act his long hair was cut off and offered to the gods. Once again, growing up was quite a definite process.

(iii) Under Roman law the year at which a boy grew up was not definitely fixed, but it was always between the ages of fourteen and seventeen. At a sacred festival in the family called the *Liberalia* he took off the *toga prætexta*, which was a toga with a narrow purple band at the foot of it and put on the *toga virilis*, which was a plain toga which adults wore. He was then conducted by his friends and relations down to the forum and formally introduced to public life. It was essentially a religious ceremony. And once again there was a quite definite day on which the lad attained manhood. There was a Roman custom that on the day a boy or girl grew up, the boy offered his ball, and the girl her doll, to Apollo to show that they had put away childish things.

When a boy was an *infant* in the eyes of the law, he might be the owner of a vast property but he could take no legal decision; he was not in control of his own life; everything was done and directed for him; and, therefore, for all practical purposes he had no more freedom than if he were a slave; but when he became a man he entered into his full inheritance.

So—Paul argues—in the childhood of the world, the law held sway. But the law was only elementary knowledge. To describe it Paul uses the word *stoicheia*. A *stoicheion* was originally a line of things; for instance, it can mean a file of soldiers. But it came to mean the ABC, and then any elementary knowledge.

It has another meaning which some would see here—the elements of which the world is composed, and in particular, the stars. The ancient world was haunted by a belief in astrology. If a man was born under a certain star his fate, they believed, was settled. Men lived under the tyranny of the stars and longed for release. Some scholars think that Paul is saying that at one time the Galatians had been tyrannised by their belief in the baleful influence of the stars. But the whole passage seems to make it necessary to take *stoicheia* in the sense of rudimentary knowledge.

Paul says that when the Galatians—and indeed all men— were mere children, they were under the tyranny of the law; then, when everything was ready, Christ came and released men from that tyranny. So now men are no longer slaves of the law; they have become sons and have entered into their inheritance. The childhood which belonged to the law should be past; the freedom of manhood has come.

The proof that we are sons comes from the instinctive cry of the heart. In man's deepest need he cries, "Father!" to God. Paul uses the double phrase, "Abba! Father!" *Abba* is the Aramaic word for Father. It must have been often on Jesus's lips, and its sound was so sacred that men kept it in the original tongue. This instinctive cry of man's heart Paul believes to be the work of the Holy Spirit. If our hearts so cry, we know that we are sons, and all the inheritance of grace is ours.

For Paul, he who governed his life by slavery to the law was still a child; he who had learned the way of grace had become a mature man in the Christian faith.

PROGRESS IN REVERSE

Galatians 4: 8–11

There was a time when you did not know God, and when you
were slaves to gods who are no gods at all; but now that you
know God—or rather now that God knows you—how can you turn
back again to the weak and poverty-stricken elementary things,
for it is to them that you wish to be enslaved all over again?
You meticulously observe days and months and seasons and years.
I am afraid for you, lest all the labour I spent on you is to go
for nothing.

PAUL is still basing on the conception that the law is an elementary stage in religion, and that the mature man is he who
takes his stand on grace. The law was all right in the old
days when they did not know any better. But now they have
come to know God and his grace. Then Paul corrects himself—man cannot by his own efforts know God; God of his
grace reveals himself to man. We can never seek God unless he
has already found us. So Paul demands, "Are you now going
back to a stage that you should have left behind long ago?"

He calls the elementary things, the religion based on law,
weak and poverty-stricken. (i) It is *weak* because it is helpless.
It can define sin; it can convict a man of sin; but it can
neither find for him forgiveness for past sin nor strength to
conquer future sin. (ii) It is *poverty-stricken* in comparison
with the splendour of grace. By its very nature the law can
deal with only one situation. For every fresh situation man
needs a fresh law; but the wonder of grace is that it is *poikilos*,
which means *variegated, many-coloured.* That is to say, there
is no possible situation in life which grace cannot match; it is
sufficient for all things.

One of the features of Jewish law was its observance of
special times. In this passage the *days* are the Sabbaths of
each week; the *months* are the new moons; the *seasons* are
the great annual feasts like the Passover, Pentecost and the
Feast of Tabernacles; the *years* are the Sabbatic years, that is,

every seventh. The failure of a religion which is dependent on special occasions is that almost inevitably it divides days into sacred and secular; and the further almost inevitable step is that when a man has meticulously observed the sacred days he is liable to think that he has discharged his duty to God.

Although that was the religion of legalism, it was very far from being the prophetic religion. It has been said that, "The ancient Hebrew people had no word in their language to correspond to the word 'religion' as it is commonly used today. The whole of life as they saw it came from God, and was subject to his law and governance. There could be no separate part of it in their thought labelled 'religion.'

"Jesus Christ did not say, 'I am come that they may have religion,' but, 'I am come that they may have life, and have it abundantly.'" To make religion a thing of special times is to make it an external thing. For the real Christian every day is God's day.

It was Paul's fear that men who had once known the splendour of grace would slip back to legalism, and that men who had once lived in the presence of God would shut him up to special days.

LOVE'S APPEAL

Galatians 4: 12–20

Brothers, I entreat you, become as I am, because I became as you are. I have no complaints against the way that once you treated me. You know that it was because I was ill that I first preached the gospel to you. It must have been a temptation to you to do so, but you did not look on me with contempt or turn with loathing from me, but you received me as if I were an angel of God, as you would have received Christ Jesus. I once had cause to congratulate you. Where has that cause gone to? I am prepared to give evidence in your favour that you would have dug out your eyes and given them to me. So then— have I become your enemy because I tell you the truth? It is not for any honourable reason that these other people pay court to you, but because they wish to put the barriers up so that you will have to pay court to them. It is always a fine thing to be zealous in a fine affair, and that not only when I am actually present with you. My little children, for whom I suffer the birth-pangs all over again, until you have taken the form of Christ, I wish I could be with you now! I wish that I had not to talk like this to you, because I am worried about you.

PAUL makes not a theological but a personal appeal. He reminds them that for their sake he had become a Gentile; he had cut adrift from the traditions in which he had been brought up and become what they are; and his appeal is that they should not seek to become Jews but might become like himself.

Here we have a reference to Paul's "thorn in the flesh." It was through illness that first he came to them. We discuss this thorn more fully when dealing with 2 *Corinthians* 12: 7. It has been held to be the persecution which he suffered, the temptations of the flesh, which he is said never to have succeeded in suppressing; his physical appearance, which the Corinthians regarded as contemptible (2 *Corinthians* 10: 10). The oldest tradition is that it was violent and prostrating headaches. From this passage itself there emerge two indications.

The Galatians would have given him their eyes if they could have done so. It has been suggested that Paul's eyes always troubled him because he had been dazzled so much on the Damascus Road that ever afterwards he could see only dimly and painfully.

The word translated *you did not turn from me with loathing* literally means *you did not spit at me*. In the ancient world it was the custom for a man to spit when he met an epileptic in order to avert the influence of the evil spirit which was believed to be resident in the sufferer; so it has been suggested that Paul was an epileptic.

If we can find out just when Paul came to Galatia, it may be possible to deduce why he came. It is possible that

Acts 13: 13, 14 describe that coming. That passage presents a problem. Paul and Barnabas and Mark had come from Cyprus to the mainland. They came to Perga in Pamphylia; there Mark left them; and then they proceeded straight to Antioch in Pisidia, which is in the province of Galatia. Why did Paul not preach in Pamphylia? It was a populous district. Why did he choose to go to Antioch in Pisidia? The road that led there, up into the central plateau, was one of the most difficult and dangerous in the world. That is perhaps why Mark went home. Why, then, this sudden flight from Pamphylia? The reason may well be that, since Pamphylia and the coastal plain were districts where malarial fever raged, Paul contracted this sickness and his only remedy would be to seek the highlands of Galatia, so that he arrived amongst the Galatians a sick man. Now this malaria recurs and is accompanied by a prostrating headache which has been likened to "a red-hot bar thrust through the forehead." It may well have been that it was this prostrating pain which was Paul's thorn in the flesh and which was torturing him when first he came to Galatia.

He talks about those who were sedulously paying court to the Galatians; he means those who were seeking to persuade them to adopt Jewish ways. If they were successful, the Galatians would in turn have to pay humble court to them to be allowed in order to be circumcised and enter the Jewish nation. Their sole purpose paid court to the Galatians, but they only did so to get control of the Galatians and reduce them to subjection to themselves and to the law.

In the end Paul uses a vivid metaphor. His bringing the Galatians to Christ cost him pain like a mother's travail; and now he has to go through it all again. Christ is in them, as it were in embryo; he has to bring them to birth.

No one can fail to see the deep affection of the last words. *My little children*—diminutives in Latin and Greek always express deep affection. John often uses this expression but Paul uses it nowhere else; his heart is running over. We do well to note that Paul did not scold with bitter words;

he yearned over his straying children. It was said of Florence
Allshorn, famous missionary and teacher, that if she had cause
to rebuke any of her students she did so, as it were, with her
arm around them. The accent of love will penetrate where
the tones of anger will never find a way.

AN OLD STORY AND A NEW MEANING

Galatians 4: 21—5: 1

> Tell me this—you who want to be subject to the law, you listen
> to it being read to you, don't you? Well, then, it stands written in it
> that Abraham had two sons; one was the son of the slave girl
> and one was the son of the free woman. But the son of the slave
> girl was born in the ordinary human way, whereas the son of the
> free woman was born through a promise. Now these things are
> an allegory. For these two women stand for two covenants. One
> of these covenants—the one which originated on Mount Sinai—
> bears children who are destined for slavery—and that one is
> represented by Hagar. Now Hagar stands for Mount Sinai, which
> is in Arabia, and corresponds to the present Jerusalem; for she
> is a slave and so are her children. But the Jerusalem which is
> above is free and she is our mother. For it stands written, "Rejoice,
> O barren one, who never bore a child; break forth into a shout
> of joy, O you who know not the pangs of bearing a child;
> for the children of her who was left alone are more than those
> of her who had a husband." But we, brothers, are in the same
> position as Isaac; we are children of promise. But in the old days
> the child who was born in the ordinary human way persecuted the
> child who was born in the spiritual way; and exactly the same
> thing happens now. But what does the scripture say? "Cast out the
> slave girl and her son, for the son of the slave girl must not
> inherit with the son of the free woman." So we, brothers, are
> children not of the slave girl but of the free woman. It is for
> this freedom that Christ has set us free. Stand, therefore, in it
> and do not get yourselves involved all over again in a slavish yoke.

WHEN we seek to interpret a passage like this we must
remember that for the devout and scholarly Jew, and especially
for the Rabbis, scripture had more than one meaning; and the
literal meaning was often regarded as the least important.

For the Jewish Rabbis a passage of scripture had four meanings. (i) *Peshat,* its simple or literal meaning. (ii) *Remaz,*
its suggested meaning. (iii) *Derush*, the meaning deduced by
investigation. (iv) *Sod*, the allegorical meaning. The first letters
of these four words—P R D S—are the consonants of the word
Paradise—and when a man had succeeded in penetrating into
these four different meanings he reached the joy of paradise!

It is to be noted that the summit of all meanings was the
allegorical meaning. It therefore often happened that the
Rabbis would take a simple bit of historical narrative from
the Old Testament and read into it inner meanings which
often appear to us fantastic but which were very convincing
to the people of their day. Paul was a trained Rabbi; and that
is what he is doing here. He takes the story involving Abraham,
Sarah, Hagar, Ishmael and Isaac (*Genesis*, chapters 16, 17, 21),
which in the Old Testament is a straightforward narrative
and he allegorises it to illustrate his point.

The outline of the story is as follows:—Abraham and Sarah
were far advanced in years and Sarah had no child. She did
what any wife would have done in those patriarchal times
and sent Abraham in to her slave girl, Hagar, to see if she
could bear a child on her behalf. Hagar had a son called
Ishmael. In the meantime God had come and promised that
Sarah would have a child, which was so difficult to believe
that it appeared impossible to Abraham and Sarah; but in
due time Isaac was born. That is to say, Ishmael was born
of the ordinary human impulses of the flesh; Isaac was born
because of God's promise; and Sarah was a free woman,
while Hagar was a slave girl. From the beginning Hagar
had been inclined to triumph over Sarah, because barrenness
was a sore shame to a woman; there was an atmosphere
charged with trouble. Later Sarah found Ishmael "mocking"
(Authorized Version) Isaac—this Paul equates with persecution—and insisted that Hagar should be cast out, so that
the child of the slave girl should not share the inheritance
with her freeborn son. Further, Arabia was regarded as the
land of slaves where the descendants of Hagar dwelt.

Paul takes that old story and allegorises it. Hagar stands for the old covenant of the law, made on Mount Sinai, which is in fact in Arabia, the land of Hagar's descendants. Hagar herself was a slave and all her children were born into slavery; and that covenant whose basis is the law turns men into slaves of the law. Hagar's child was born from merely human impulses; and legalism is the best that man can do. On the other hand Sarah stands for the new covenant in Jesus Christ, God's new way of dealing with men not by law but by grace. Her child was born free—and according to God's promise—and all his descendants must be free. As the child of the slave girl persecuted the child of the free woman, the children of law now persecute the children of grace and promise. But as in the end the child of the slave girl was cast out and had no share in the inheritance, so in the end those who are legalists will be cast out from God and have no share in the inheritance of grace.

Strange as all this may seem to us, it enshrines one great truth. The man who makes law the principle of his life is in the position of a slave; whereas the man who makes grace the principle of his life is free, for, as a great saint put it, the Christian's maxim is, "Love God and do what you like." It is the power of that love, and not the constraint of law, that will keep us right; for love is always more powerful than law.

THE PERSONAL RELATIONSHIP

Galatians 5: 1–12

Look now—it is I, Paul, who am speaking to you—I tell you that if you get yourself circumcised Christ is no good to you. Again I give my word to every man who gets himself circumcised that he is under obligation to keep the whole law. You who seek to get yourselves right with God by means of legalism have got yourself into a position in which you have rendered ineffective all that Christ did for you. You have fallen from grace. For it is by the Spirit and by faith that we eagerly expect the hope of being right with God. For in Jesus Christ it is not of the slightest importance whether a man is circumcised or uncircumcised. What does matter is faith which works through love. You were running well. Who put up a road-block to stop you obeying the truth? The persuasion which is being exercised on you just now is not from him who calls you. A little leaven leavens the whole lump. I have confidence in you in the Lord; I am sure that you will take no other view. He who is upsetting you—whoever he is—will bear his own judgment. As for me, brothers, if I am still preaching that circumcision is necessary, why am I still being persecuted? So the stumbling-block of the Cross is removed, is it? I wish that those who are upsetting you would get themselves not only circumcised but castrated!

It was Paul's position that the way of grace and the way of law were mutually exclusive. The way of law makes salvation dependent on human achievement; the man who takes the way of grace simply casts himself and his sin upon the mercy of God. Paul went on to argue that if you accepted circumcision, that is to say, if you accepted one part of the law, logically you had to accept the whole law.

Suppose a man desires to become a naturalized subject of a country and carefully carries out all the rules and regulations of that country as they affect naturalization. He cannot stop there but is bound to accept *all* the other rules and regulations as well. So Paul argued that if a man were circumcised he had put himself under an obligation to the whole law to which circumcision was the introduction; and, if he took that way, he had automatically turned his back on the way of grace, and, as far as he was concerned, Christ might never have died.

To Paul all that mattered was faith which works through love. That is just another way of saying that the essence of Christianity is not law but a personal relationship to Jesus Christ. The Christian's faith is founded not on a book but on a person; its dynamic is not obedience to any law but love to Jesus Christ.

Once, the Galatians had known that, but now they were turning back to the law. "A little leaven," said Paul, "leavens the whole lump." For the Jew leaven nearly always stood for evil influence. What Paul is saying is, "This legalistic movement may not have gone very far yet, but you must root it out before it destroys your whole religion."

Paul ends with a very blunt saying. Galatia was near Phrygia and the great worship of that part of the world was of Cybele. It was the practice that priests and really devout worshippers of Cybele mutilated themselves by castration. Paul says, "If you go on in this way, of which circumcision is the beginning, you might as well end up by castrating yourselves like these heathen priests." It is a grim illustration at which a polite society raises its eyebrows, but it would be intensely real to the Galatians who knew all about the priests of Cybele.

CHRISTIAN FREEDOM

Galatians 5: 13–15

As for you, brothers, it was for freedom that you were called, only you must not use this freedom as a bridgehead through which the worst side of human nature can invade you, but in love you must serve one another; for the whole law stands complete in one word, in the sentence, "You must love your neighbour as yourself." But if you snap at one another, and devour one another, you must watch that you do not end up by wiping each other out.

WITH this paragraph Paul's letter changes its emphasis. Up to this point it has been theological; now it becomes intensely ethical. Paul had a characteristically practical mind. Even when he has been scaling the highest heights of thought he always ends a letter on a practical note. To him a theology was not the slightest use unless it could be lived out. In *Romans* he wrote one of the world's great theological treatises, and then, quite suddenly, in the 12th chapter the theology came down to earth and issued in the most practical advice. Vincent Taylor once said, "The test of a good theologian is, can he write a tract?" That is to say, after his flights of thought can he reduce it all to something that the ordinary man can understand and do? Paul always triumphantly satisfies that test, just as here the whole matter is brought to the acid test of daily living.

His theology always ran one danger. When he declared that the end of the reign of law had come and that the reign of grace had arrived, it was always possible for someone to say, "That, then, means that I can do what I like; all the restraints are lifted and I can follow my inclinations wherever they lead me. Law is gone and grace ensures forgiveness anyway." But to the end of the day there remained for Paul two obligations. (i) One he does not mention here but it is implicit in all his thinking. It is *the obligation to God.* If God loved us like that then the love of Christ constrains us. I cannot soil a life which God paid for with his own life. (ii) There is the *obligation to our fellow men.* We are free, but our freedom loves its neighbour as itself.

The names of the different forms of government are suggestive. *Monarchy* is government by one, and began in the interests of efficiency, for government by committees has always had its drawbacks. *Oligarchy* means government by the few and can be justified by arguing that only the few are fit to govern. *Aristocracy* means government by the best, but *best* is left to be defined. *Plutocracy* means government by the wealthy and is justified by the claim that those who have the biggest stake in the country have a logical right to rule it. *Democracy* means government of the people, by the people, for the people. Christianity is the only true democracy, because in a Christian state everyone would think as much of his neighbour as he does of himself. Christian freedom is not licence, for the simple but tremendous reason that the Christian is not a man who has become free to sin, but a man, who, by the grace of God, has become free *not to sin.*

Paul adds a grim bit of advice. "Unless," he says, "you

solve the problem of living together you will make life impossible." Selfishness in the end does not exalt a man; it destroys him.

THE EVIL THINGS

Galatians 5: 16–21

> I tell you, let your walk and conversation be dominated by the Spirit, and don't let the desires of the lower side of your nature have their way. For the desires of the lower side of human nature are the very reverse of the desires of the Spirit, and the desires of the Spirit are the very reverse of those of the lower side of human nature, for these are fundamentally opposed to each other, so that you cannot do whatever you like. The deeds of the lower side of human nature are obvious—fornication, impurity, wantonness, idolatry, witchcraft, enmity, strife, jealousy, uncontrolled temper, self-seeking, dissension, heretical division, envy, drunkenness, carousing, and all that is like these things. I warn you, as I have warned you before, that those who do things like that will not inherit the Kingdom of God.

No man was ever more conscious of the tension in human nature than Paul. As the soldier in Studdert Kennedy's poem said;

> I'm a man and a man's a mixture
> Right down from his very birth;
> For part of him comes from heaven,
> And part of him comes from earth.

For Paul it was essential that Christian freedom should mean not freedom to indulge the lower side of human nature, but freedom to walk in the life of the Spirit. He gives us a catalogue of evil things. Every word he uses has a picture behind it.

Fornication; it has been said, and said truly, that the one completely new virtue Christianity brought into the world was chastity. Christianity came into a world where sexual immorality was not only condoned, but was regarded as essential to the ordinary working of life.

Impurity; the word that Paul uses (*akatharsia*) is interesting. It can be used for the pus of an unclean wound, for a tree that has never been pruned, for material which has never been sifted. In its positive form (*katharos*, an adjective meaning *pure*) it is commonly used in housing contracts to describe a house that is left clean and in good condition. But its most suggestive use is that *katharos* is used of that ceremonial cleanness which entitles a man to approach his gods. Impurity, then, is that which makes a man unfit to come before God, the soiling of life with the things which separate us from him.

Wantonness; this word (*aselgeia*) is translated licentiousness in the Revised Standard Version (*Mark* 7: 22; 2 *Corinthians* 12: 21; *Galatians* 5: 19; *Ephesians* 4: 19; 1 *Peter* 4: 3; *Jude* 4; *Romans* 13: 13 and 2 *Peter* 2: 18). It has been defined as "readiness for any pleasure." The man who practises it has been said to know no restraint, but to do whatever caprice and wanton insolence may suggest. Josephus ascribed it to Jezebel when she built a temple to Baal in Jerusalem. The idea is that of a man who is so far gone in desire that he has ceased to care what people say or think.

Idolatry; this means the worship of gods which the hands of men have made. It is the sin in which material things have taken the place of God.

Witchcraft; this literally means *the use of drugs*. It can mean the beneficent use of drugs by a doctor; but it can also mean *poisoning*, and it came to be very specially connected with the use of drugs for sorcery, of which the ancient world was full.

Enmity; the idea is that of the man who is characteristically hostile to his fellow men; it is the precise opposite of the Christian virtue of love for the brethren and for all men.

Strife; originally this word had mainly to do with *the rivalry for prizes*. It can even be used in a good sense in that connection, but much more commonly it means the rivalry which has found its outcome in quarrellings and wrangling.

Jealousy; this word (*zelos* from which our word *zeal* comes) was originally a good word. It meant *emulation*, the desire to attain to nobility when we see it. But it degenerated; came to mean the desire to have what someone else has, wrong desire for what is not for us.

Uncontrolled temper; the word Paul uses means bursts of temper. It describes not an anger which lasts but anger which flames out and then dies.

Self-seeking; this word has a very illuminating history. It is *eritheia* and originally meant *the work of a hired labourer* (*erithos*). So it came to mean *work done for pay*. It went on to mean *canvassing for political or public office,* and it describes the man who wants office, not from any motives of service, but for what he can get out of it.

Dissension; literally the word means *a standing apart.* After one of his great victories Nelson attributed it to the fact that he had the happiness to command a band of brothers. *Dissension* describes a society in which the very opposite is the case, where the members fly apart instead of coming together.

Heretical division; this might be described as crystallized dissension. The word is *hairesis,* from which comes our word *heresy. Hairesis* was not originally a bad word at all. It comes from a root which means *to choose,* and it was used for a philosopher's school of followers or for any band of people who shared a common belief. The tragedy of life is that people who hold different views very often finish up by disliking, not each others' views, but each other. It should be possible to differ with a man and yet remain friends.

Envy; this word (*phthonos*), is a mean word. Euripides called it "the greatest of all diseases among men." The essence of it is that it does not describe the spirit which desires, nobly or ignobly, to have what someone else has; it describes the spirit which grudges the fact that the other person has these things at all. It does not so much want the things for itself; it merely wants to take them from the other. The Stoics defined it as "grief at someone else's good." Basil called it "grief at your neighbour's good fortune." It is the quality, not so much of the jealous, but rather of the embittered mind.

Drunkenness; in the ancient world this was not a common

vice. The Greeks drank more wine than they did milk; even
children drank wine. But they drank it in the proportion of
three parts of water to two of wine. Greek and Christian
alike would have condemned drunkenness as a thing which
turned a man into a beast.

Carousing; this word (*komos*) has an interesting history.
A *komos* was a band of friends who accompanied a victor of
the games after his victory. They danced and laughed and
sang his praises. It also described the bands of the devotees
of Bacchus, god of wine. It describes what in regency England
would have been called a *rout*. It means unrestrained revelry,
enjoyment that has degenerated into licence.

When we get to the root meaning of these words, we see
that life has not changed so very much.

THE LOVELY THINGS

Galatians 5: 22-26

> But the fruit of the Spirit is love, joy, peace, patience, kindness,
> goodness, fidelity, gentleness, self-control. There is no law which
> condemns things like that. Those who belong to Jesus Christ have
> crucified their own unregenerate selves along with all their passions
> and their desires.
>
> If we are living in the Spirit let us also keep step with the
> Spirit. Don't become seekers after empty reputation; don't provoke
> each other; don't envy each other.

As in the previous verses Paul set out the evil things characteristic of the flesh, so now he sets out the lovely things which
are the fruit of the Spirit. Again it is worth while to look at each
word separately.

Love; the New Testament word for *love* is *agape*. This is
not a word which classical Greek uses commonly. In Greek
there are four words for love. (*a*) *Eros* means the love of a
man for a maid; it is the love which has passion in it. It
is never used in the New Testament at all. (*b*) *Philia* is the

warm love which we feel for our nearest and our dearest; it is a thing of the heart. (c) *Storge* rather means affection and is specially used of the love of parents and children. (d) *Agape*, the Christian word, means unconquerable benevolence. It means that no matter what a man may do to us by way of insult or injury or humiliation we will never seek anything else but his highest good. It is therefore a feeling of the mind as much as of the heart; it concerns the will as much as the emotions. It describes the deliberate effort—which we can make only with the help of God—never to seek anything but the best even for those who seek the worst for us.

Joy; the Greek is *chara*, and the characteristic of this word is that it most often describes that joy which has a basis in religion (cp. *Psalm* 30: 11; *Romans* 14: 17; 15: 13; *Philippians* 1: 4, 25). It is not the joy that comes from earthly things, still less from triumphing over someone else in competition. It is a joy whose foundation is God.

Peace; in contemporary colloquial Greek this word (*eirene*) had two interesting usages. It was used of the serenity which a country enjoyed under the just and beneficent government of a good emperor; and it was used of the good order of a town or village. Villages had an official who was called the superintendent of the village's *eirene*, the keeper of the public peace. Usually in the New Testament *eirene* stands for the Hebrew *shalom* and means not just freedom from trouble but everything that makes for a man's highest good. Here it means that tranquillity of heart which derives from the all-pervading consciousness that our times are in the hands of God. It is interesting to note that *Chara* and *Eirene* both became very common Christian names in the Church.

Makrothumia; this is a great word. The writer of First Maccabees (8: 4) says that it was by *makrothumia* that the Romans became masters of the world, and by that he means the Roman persistence which would never make peace with an enemy even in defeat, a kind of conquering patience. Generally speaking the word is not used of patience in regard to things or events but in regard to people. Chrysostom said that it is the grace of the man who could revenge himself and does not, the man who is slow to wrath. The most illuminating thing about it is that it is commonly used in the New Testament of the attitude of God towards men (*Romans* 2: 4; 9: 22; 1 *Timothy* 1: 16; 1 *Peter* 3: 20). If God had been a man, he would have wiped out this world long ago; but he has that patience which bears with all our sinning and will not cast us off. In our dealings with our fellow men we must reproduce this loving, forbearing, forgiving, patient attitude of God towards ourselves.

Kindness and *goodness* are closely connected words. For *kindness* the word is *chrestotes*. It, too, is commonly translated *goodness*. The Rheims version of 2 *Corinthians* 6: 6 translates it *sweetness*. It is a lovely word. Plutarch says that it has a far wider place than justice. Old wine is called *chrestos, mellow*. Christ's yoke is called *chrestos* (*Matthew* 11: 30), that is, it does not chafe. The whole idea of the word is a goodness which is kind. The word Paul uses for *goodness* (*agathosune*) is a peculiarly Bible word and does not occur in secular Greek (*Romans* 15: 14; *Ephesians* 5: 9; 2 *Thessalonians* 1: 11). It is the widest word for goodness; it is defined as "virtue equipped at every point." What is the difference? *Agathosune* might, and could, rebuke and discipline; *chrestotes* can only help. Trench says that Jesus showed *agathosune* when he cleansed the Temple and drove out those who were making it a bazaar; but he showed *chrestotes* when he was kind to the sinning woman who anointed his feet. The Christian needs that goodness which at one and the same time can be kind and strong.

Fidelity; this word (*pistis*) is common in secular Greek for *trustworthiness*. It is the characteristic of the man who is reliable.

Gentleness; praotes is the most untranslatable of words. In the New Testament it has three main meanings. (*a*) It means *being submissive to the will of God* (*Matthew* 5: 5; 11: 29; 21: 5). (*b*) It means *being teachable,* being not too proud to learn (*James* 1: 21). (*c*) Most often of all it means *being considerate* (1 *Corinthians* 4: 21; 2 *Corinthians* 10: 1; *Ephesians* 4: 2). Aristotle defined *praotes* as the mean between excessive anger and excessive angerlessness, the quality of the man who is always angry at the right time and never at the wrong time. What throws most light on its meaning is that the adjective *praus* is used of an animal that has been tamed and brought under control; and so the word speaks of that self-control which Christ alone can give.

Self-control; the word is *egkrateia* which Plato uses of *self-mastery.* It is the spirit which has mastered its desires and its love of pleasure. It is used of the athlete's discipline of his body (1 *Corinthians* 9: 25) and of the Christian's mastery of sex (1 *Corinthians* 7: 9). Secular Greek uses it of the virtue of an Emperor who never lets his private interests influence the government of his people. It is the virtue which makes a man so master of himself that he is fit to be the servant of others.

It was Paul's belief and experience that the Christian died with Christ and rose again to a life, new and clean, in which the evil things of the old self were gone and the lovely things of the Spirit had come to fruition.

BURDEN-BEARING

Galatians 6: 1–5

> Brothers, if a man is caught out in some moral slip-up, you whose lives are dominated by the Spirit must correct such a man with the spirit of gentleness, and, as you do it, you must think about yourselves, in case you too should be tempted. Carry one another's burdens, and so fulfil the law of Christ. For, if anyone thinks of himself as important while he is of no importance, he is deceiving himself with the fancies of his mind. Let every man test his own work, and then any ground of boasting that he has will be in regard to himself and not in comparison with others. For each man must carry his own pack.

PAUL knew the problems that arise in any Christian society.

The best of men slip up. The word Paul uses (*paraptoma*) does not mean a deliberate sin; but a slip as might come to a man on an icy road or a dangerous path. Now, the danger of those who are really trying to live the Christian life is that they are apt to judge the sins of others hardly. There is an element of hardness in many a good man. There are many good people to whom you could not go and sob out a story of failure and defeat; they would be bleakly unsympathetic. But Paul says that, if a man does make a slip, the real Christian duty is to get him on his feet again. The word he uses for *to correct* is used for executing a repair and also for the work of a surgeon in removing some growth from a man's body or in setting a broken limb. The whole atmosphere of the word lays the stress not on punishment but on cure; the correction is thought of not as a penalty but as an amendment. And Paul goes on to say that when we see a man fall into a fault we do well to say, "There but for the grace of God go I."

He goes on to rebuke conceit and gives a recipe whereby it may well be avoided. We are to compare our achievement not with the work of our neighbours but with what our best would have been. When we do that, there can never be any cause for conceit.

Twice in this passage Paul speaks about bearing burdens. There is a kind of burden which comes to a man from the chances and the changes of life; it is fulfilling the law of Christ to help everyone who has such a burden to carry. But there is also a burden which a man must bear himself. The word Paul uses is the word for a soldier's pack. There is a duty which none can do for us and a task for which we must be personally responsible.

KEEPING IT UP

Galatians 6: 6–10

He who is being instructed in the word must share in all good things with him who is giving instruction. Don't deceive yourselves;

no one can make a fool of God; whatever a man sows this he will also reap. He who sows to his own lower nature will from that nature reap a blighted harvest. He who sows to the Spirit will from the Spirit reap life eternal. Don't get tired of doing the fine thing, for, when the proper time comes, we will reap so long as we don't relax our efforts. So then, as we have opportunity, let us do good to all, especially to those who are members of the household of the faith.

HERE Paul becomes intensely practical.

The Christian Church had its teachers. In those days the Church was a really sharing institution. No Christian could bear to have too much while others had too little. So Paul says, "If a man is teaching you the eternal truths, the least you can do is share with him such material things as you possess."

He goes on to state a grim truth. He insists that life holds the scales with an even balance. If a man allows the lower side of his nature to dominate him, in the end he can expect nothing but a harvest of trouble. But if he keeps on walking the high way and doing the fine thing, in the end God will repay.

Christianity never took the threat out of life. The Greeks believed in Nemesis; they believed that, when a man did a wrong thing, immediately Nemesis was on his trail and sooner or later caught up. All Greek tragedy is a sermon on the text, "The doer shall suffer." What we do not sufficiently remember is this—it is blessedly true that God can and does forgive men for their sins, but not even he can wipe out the consequence of sin. If a man sins against his body, soon or late he will pay in ruined health—even if he is forgiven. If a man sins against his loved ones, soon or late hearts will be broken—even if he is forgiven. John B. Gough, the great temperance orator, who had lived a reckless early life, used to declare in warning, "The scars remain." And Origen, the great Christian scholar and a universalist, believed that, although all men would be saved, even then the marks of sin would remain. We cannot trade on the forgiveness of God. There is a moral law in the universe. If a man breaks it he may be forgiven, but, nonetheless, he breaks it at his peril.

Paul finishes by reminding his friends that sometimes the duty of generosity may be irksome, but no man who ever cast his bread upon the waters found that it did not return some day to him.

THE CLOSING WORDS

Galatians 6: 11–18

> See in what large letters I am writing in my own handwriting. Those who wish to make a pretentious display from the merely human point of view are trying to compel you to get yourselves circumcised, but their real object is to avoid persecution because of the Cross of Christ. For those who advocate circumcision do not themselves keep the law, but they wish you to get yourselves circumcised that they may boast about the way in which you are observing the outward and the human rituals. God forbid that I should boast except in the Cross of our Lord Jesus Christ through whom the world has been crucified to me and I to the world. To be circumcised is of no importance, and to be uncircumcised makes no difference. What does matter is to be re-created. May peace and mercy be upon all who shall walk by this standard and on the Israel of God. For the future, let no one trouble me for I bear the brands of Jesus in my body.
>
> Brothers, the grace of the Lord Jesus Christ be with your spirit. So let it be.

ORDINARILY Paul added only his signature to the letter which the scribe wrote to his dictation; but in this case his heart is running over with such love and anxiety for the Galatians that he writes this whole last paragraph. "See," he says, "in what large letters I am writing in my own handwriting." The large letters may be due to three things. (*a*) This paragraph may be written large because of its importance, as if it were printed in heavy type. (*b*) It may be written large because Paul was unused to wielding a pen and it was the best that he could do. (c) It may be that Paul's eyes were weak, or that the blinding headache was on him, and all he could produce was the large sprawling handwriting of a man who can hardly see.

He comes back to the centre of the matter. Those who wanted the Galatians to get themselves circumcised did so for three reasons. (a) It would save them from persecution. The Romans recognized the Jewish religion and officially allowed Jews to practise it. Circumcision was the unanswerable mark of a Jew; and so these people saw in it a passport to safety should persecution arise. Circumcision would keep them safe from the hatred of the Jews and the law of Rome alike. (b) In the last analysis, by circumcision and by keeping the rules and regulations of the law, they were trying to put on a show that would win the approval of God. Paul, however, was quite certain that nothing that man could do could win salvation; so once again, pointing them to the Cross, he summons them to cease trying to earn salvation and to trust to the grace which loved them like that. (c) Those who desired the Galatians to be circumcised did not themselves keep all the law. No man could. But they wanted to boast about the Galatians as their latest trophies. They wanted to glory in their power over people whom they had reduced to their own legalistic slavery. So Paul once again lays it down with all the intensity of which he is capable that circumcision and uncircumcision do not matter; what does matter is that act of faith in Christ which opens a new life to a man.

"I bear," said Paul, "the brands of Jesus in my body." There are two possible meanings of this. (a) The *stigmata* have always fascinated men. It is told of Francis of Assisi that once as he fasted on a lonely mountain top he seemed to see the love of God crucified on a Cross that stretched across the whole horizon and as he saw it a sword of grief and pity pierced his heart. Slowly the vision faded and Francis relaxed; and then, they say, he looked down and lo! the marks of the nails were in his hands and he bore them to the end of his days. Whether it is truth or legend we cannot tell, for there are more things in this world than our matter-of-fact philosophy dreams of; and some think that Paul had so really passed through an experience of crucifixion with his Lord that he, too, bore the print of the nails in his hands. (*b*) Often a master branded his slaves with a mark that showed them to be his. Most likely what Paul means is that the scars of the things he had suffered for Christ are the brands which show him to be Christ's slave. In the end it is not his apostolic authority that he uses as a basis of appeal; it is the wounds he sustained for Christ's sake. Like Mr Valiant-for-Truth Paul said, "My marks and scars I carry with me to be my witness to him who will now be my rewarder."

After the storm and stress and intensity of the letter comes the peace of the benediction. Paul has argued and rebuked and cajoled but his last word is GRACE, for him the only word that really mattered.

THE LETTER TO THE EPHESIANS

INTRODUCTION TO THE LETTER TO
THE EPHESIANS

THE SUPREME LETTER

By common consent the *Letter to the Ephesians* ranks very high in the devotional and theological literature of the Christian Church. It has been called "The Queen of the Epistles"— and rightly so. Many would hold that it is indeed the highest reach of New Testament thought. When John Knox was very near his end, the book that was most often read to him was John Calvin's *Sermons on the Letter to the Ephesians.* Coleridge said of *Ephesians* that it was "the divinest composition of man." He went on: "It embraces first, those doctrines peculiar to Christianity, and, then, those precepts common with it in natural religion." *Ephesians* clearly has a place all its own in the Pauline correspondence.

And yet there are certain very real problems connected with it. These problems are not the product of the minds of over-critical scholars, but are plain for all to see. When, however, these problems are solved, *Ephesians* becomes a greater letter than ever and shines with an even more radiant light.

THE CIRCUMSTANCES OF THE WRITING OF EPHESIANS

Before we turn to the doubtful things, let us set down the certainties. First, *Ephesians* was clearly written when Paul was in prison. He calls himself "a prisoner for Christ" (3: 1); it is as "a prisoner for the Lord" that he beseeches them (4: 1); he is "an ambassador in chains" (6: 20). It was in prison, and very near to the end, that Paul wrote *Ephesians.*

Second, *Ephesians* has clearly a close connection with *Colossians.* It would seem that Tychicus was the bearer of both these letters. In *Colossians* Paul says that Tychicus will tell them all about his affairs (*Colossians* 4: 7); and in

Ephesians he says that Tychicus will give them all information (*Ephesians* 6: 21). Further, there is a close resemblance between the substance of the two letters, so close that more than 55 verses in the two letters are verbatim the same. Either, as Coleridge held, *Colossians* is what might be called "the overflow" of *Ephesians*, or *Ephesians* is a greater version of *Colossians*. We shall in the end come to see that it is this resemblance which gives us the clue to the unique place of *Ephesians* among the letters of Paul.

THE PROBLEM

So, then, it is certain that *Ephesians* was written when Paul was in prison for the faith and that it has in some way the closest possible connection with *Colossians*. The problem emerges when we begin to examine the question of *to whom Ephesians was written.*

In the ancient days letters were written on rolls of papyrus. When finished, they were tied with thread, and, if they were specially private or important, the knots in the thread were then sealed. But it was seldom that any address was written on them, for the very simple reason that, for the ordinary individual, there was no postal system. There was a government post, but it was available only for official and imperial correspondence and not for the ordinary person. Letters in those days were delivered by hand and therefore no address was necessary. So the titles of the New Testament letters are not part of the original letters at all. They were inserted afterwards when the letters were collected and published for all the Church to read.

When we study *Ephesians* closely, we find it in the last degree unlikely that it was written to the church at Ephesus. There are *internal* reasons for arriving at that conclusion.

(*a*) The letter was written to Gentiles. The recipients were "Gentiles in the flesh, called the uncircumcision by what is called the circumcision, separated from Christ, alienated from the commonwealth of Israel, and strangers to the covenants of promise" (2: 11). Paul urges them "no longer to live as the

Gentiles do" (4: 17). The fact that they were Gentiles did not of itself mean that the letter could not have been written to Ephesus; but it is a fact to note.

(*b*) *Ephesians* is the most impersonal letter Paul ever wrote. It is entirely without personal greetings and without the intimate personal messages of which the other letters are so full. That is doubly surprising when we remember that Paul spent longer in Ephesus than in any other city, no less than three years (*Acts* 20: 31). Further, there is no more intimate and affectionate passage in the whole New Testament than *Acts* 20: 17–35 where we have Paul's farewell talk to the elders of Ephesus, before he left Miletus on his last journey. It is very difficult to believe in face of all this that Paul would have sent a letter to Ephesus which was so impersonal.

(*c*) The indication of the letter is that Paul and the recipients did not know each other personally and that their knowledge of each other came by hearsay. In 1: 15 Paul writes: "Because I have *heard* of your faith in the Lord Jesus." The loyalty of the people to whom he was writing was something which had come to him by information and not by experience. In 3: 2 he writes to them: "Assuming that you have heard of the stewardship of God's grace that was given to me for you." That is to say: "If you have heard that God gave me the special task and office of being the apostle to Gentiles such as you." The Church's knowledge of Paul as the apostle to the Gentiles was something of which they have heard, but not something which they knew by personal contact with him. So, then, within itself the letter bears signs that it does not fit the close and personal relationship which Paul had with the Church at Ephesus.

These facts might be explained; but there is one external fact which settles the matter. In 1: 1 none of the great early manuscripts of the Greek New Testament contain the words *in Ephesus*. They all read: "Paul . . . to the saints who are also faithful in Christ Jesus." And we know, from the way in which they comment on it, that that was the form in which the early Greek fathers knew the text.

WAS PAUL THE AUTHOR?

Some scholars have gone on to find still another difficulty in *Ephesians*. They have doubted whether Paul was the author of the letter at all. On what grounds do they base their doubts?

They say that the *vocabulary* is different from the vocabulary of Paul; and it is true that there are some seventy words in *Ephesians* which are not found in any other letter written by Paul. That need not trouble us, for the fact is that in *Ephesians* Paul was saying things which he had never said before. He was travelling a road of thought along which he had not before travelled; and naturally he needed new words to express new thoughts. It would be ridiculous to demand that a man with a mind like Paul's should never add to his vocabulary and should always express himself in the same way.

They say that the *style* is not the style of Paul. It is true—we can see it even in the English, let alone in the Greek—that the style of *Ephesians* is different from that of the other letters. The other letters are all written to meet a definite situation. But, as A. H. M'Neile has said, *Ephesians* is "a theological tract, or rather a religious mediation." Even the use of language is different. Moffatt puts it this way—generally speaking, Paul's language pours out like a torrent; but in *Ephesians* we have "a slow, bright stream, flowing steadily along, which brims its high banks." The length of the sentences in *Ephesians* is astonishing. In the Greek *Ephesians* 1: 3–14, 15–23; 2: 1–9; 3: 1–7 are each one long, meandering sentence. M'Neile very beautifully and rightly calls *Ephesians* "a poem in prose." All this is very unlike Paul's normal style.

What is to be said to this? There is first the general fact that no great writer always writes in the same style. Shakespeare can produce the very different styles of *Hamlet*, *A Midsummer Night's Dream*, *The Taming of the Shrew* and the *Sonnets*. Any great stylist—and Paul was a great stylist—writes in a style to fit his aim and his circumstances at the time of writing. It is bad criticism to say that Paul did not write *Ephesians* simply because he has evolved a new vocabulary and a new style.

But there is more. Let us remember how Paul wrote most of his letters. He wrote them in the midst of a busy ministry, when, for the most part, he was on the road. He wrote them to meet a demanding problem which had to be dealt with at the moment. That is to say, in most of his letters Paul was writing against time. Now let us remember that Paul, if he wrote *Ephesians*, wrote it *when he was in prison*. That is to say, he had all the time in the world to write it. Is it any wonder that the style of *Ephesians* is not the style of the earlier letters?

Moreover, this difference in style, this meditative, poetical quality is most apparent in the first three chapters, and they are *one long prayer*, culminating in a great doxology. There is in fact nothing like this in all Paul's letters. This is the language of lyrical prayer, not the language of argument or controversy or rebuke.

The differences are far from proving that *Ephesians* is not by Paul.

THE THOUGHT OF THE EPISTLE

Certain scholars wish to go on to say that the thought of *Ephesians* is beyond the thought of any of the other letters of Paul. Let us see what that thought is. We have seen that *Ephesians* is intimately connected with *Colossians* whose central thought is *the all-sufficiency of Jesus Christ*. In Jesus Christ were hidden all the treasures of wisdom and knowledge (*Colossians* 2:3); all the fulness of God dwelt in him (*Colossians* 1:19); in him the whole fulness of deity dwells bodily (*Colossians* 2:9); he alone is necessary and sufficient for man's salvation (*Colossians* 1:14). The whole thought of *Colossians* is based on the complete sufficiency of Jesus Christ.

The thought of *Ephesians* is a development of that conception. It is summarized in two verses of the first chapter, in which Paul speaks of God as, "having made known to us in all wisdom and insight the mystery of his will, according to his purpose which he set forth in Christ as a plan for the fulness of time, to unite all things in him, things in heaven and things on earth." (*Ephesians* 1 : 9, 10).

The key thought of *Ephesians* is the gathering together of all things in Jesus Christ. In nature as it is without Christ there is nothing but disunity and disharmony; it is "red in tooth and claw." Man's dominion has broken the social union which should exist between man and the beasts; man is divided from man; class from class; nation from nation; ideology from ideology; Gentile from Jew. What is true of the world of outer nature is true of human nature. In every man there is a tension; every man is a walking civil war, torn between the desire for good and the desire for evil; he hates his sins and loves them at one and the same time. According to both Greek and Jewish thought in the time of Paul, this disharmony extends even to the heavenly places. A cosmic battle is raging between the powers of evil and the powers of good; between God and the demons. Worst of all there is disharmony between God and man. Man, who was meant to be in fellowship with God, is estranged from him.

So, then, in this world without Christ, there is nothing but disunity. That disunity is not God's purpose but it can become a unity only when all things are united in Christ. As E. F. Scott has it: "The innumerable broken strands were to be brought together in Christ, knotted again into one, as they had been in the beginning." The central thought of *Ephesians* is the realization of the disunity in the universe and the conviction that it can become unity only when everything is united in Christ.

THE ORIGIN OF PAUL'S THOUGHT

How did Paul arrive at this great conception of the unity of all things in Jesus Christ? Most likely he came to it in two ways. It is surely the inevitable outcome of his conviction, stated so vividly in *Colossians*, that Christ is all-sufficient. But it may well be that there was something else which moved Paul's mind in this direction. He was a Roman citizen and proud of it. In his journeys Paul had seen a great deal of the Roman Empire, and now he was in Rome, the imperial city. In the Roman Empire a new unity had come to the world. The *pax Romana*, the Roman peace, was a very real thing. Kingdoms and states and countries, which had struggled and warred with each other, were gathered into a new unity in the Empire which was Rome. It may well be that in his imprisonment Paul saw with new eyes how all this unity centred in Rome; and it may well have seemed to him a symbol of how all things must centre in Christ, if a disunited nature and world and humanity were ever to be gathered into a unity. Surely, so far from being a conception that was beyond his thinking, all Paul's thinking and experience would lead him precisely to that.

THE FUNCTION OF THE CHURCH

It is in the first three chapters of the letter that Paul deals with this conception of the unity in Christ. In the second three chapters he has much to say of the place of the Church in God's plan to bring about that unity. It is here that Paul strikes out one of his greatest phrases. The Church is the *Body of Christ*. The Church is to be hands to do Christ's work, feet to run upon his errands, a mouth to speak for him. So, then, we have a double thesis in *Ephesians*. First, Christ is God's instrument of reconciliation. Second, the Church is Christ's instrument of reconciliation. The Church must bring Christ to the world; and it is within the Church that all the middle walls of separation must be broken down. It is through the Church that the unity of all the discordant elements must be achieved. As E. F. Scott has it: "The Church stands for that purpose of world-wide reconciliation for which Christ appeared, and in all their intercourse with one another Christians must seek to realize this formative idea of the Church."

WHO BUT PAUL?

This is the thought of *Ephesians*. As we have seen, there

are some who, thinking of the vocabulary and the style and the thought of this letter, cannot believe that Paul wrote it. E. J. Goodspeed, the American scholar, has put forward an interesting—but unconvincing—theory. The probability is that it was in Ephesus about the year A.D. 90 that the letters of Paul were first collected and sent out to the Church at large. It is Goodspeed's theory that the man responsible for that collection, some disciple of Paul, wrote *Ephesians* as a kind of introduction to the whole collection. Surely that theory breaks down on one salient fact. Any imitation is inferior to the original. But so far from being inferior *Ephesians* might well be said to be the greatest of all the Pauline letters. If Paul did not write it himself, we have to postulate as its writer someone who was possibly greater than Paul. E. F. Scott very relevantly demands: "Can we believe that in the Church of Paul's day there was an unknown teacher of this supreme excellence? The natural assumption is surely that an epistle so like the work of Paul at his best was written by no other man than by Paul himself." No man ever had a greater vision of Christ than this which sees in Christ the one centre in whom all the disunities of life are gathered into one. No man ever had a greater vision of the Church than this which sees in the Church God's instrument in that world-wide reconciliation. And we may well believe that no man other than Paul could rise to a vision like that.

THE DESTINATION OF EPHESIANS

We must now return to the problem which earlier we left unsolved. If *Ephesians* was not written to Ephesus—to what church was it written?

The oldest suggestion is that it was written to *Laodicea*. In *Colossians* 4: 16 Paul writes: "And when this letter has been read among you, have it read also in the church of the Laodiceans; and see that you read also the letter from Laodicea." That sentence makes certain that a letter had gone from Paul to the church at Laodicea. We possess no such letter amongst Paul's letters as they stand. Marcion was one of the first people to make a collection of Paul's letters, just about the middle of the second century, and he actually calls *Ephesians* the Letter to the Laodiceans. So from very early times there must have been a feeling in the Church that *Ephesians* was actually sent in the first instance to Laodicea.

If we accept that interesting and attractive suggestion, we still have to explain how the letter lost its individual address to Laodicea and came to be connected with Ephesus. There could be two explanations.

It may be that, when Paul died, the church at Ephesus knew that the church at Laodicea possessed a wonderful letter from Paul; and wrote to Laodicea asking for a copy. A copy may have been made and sent off, omitting only the words *in Laodicea* in the first verse, and leaving a blank as the earliest manuscripts have a blank there. Almost thirty years later the letters of Paul were collected for general publication. Now Laodicea was in a district which was notorious for earthquakes, and it may well have been that all its archives were destroyed; and that, therefore, when the collection was made, the only copy of the Letter to the Laodiceans was that which survived in Ephesus. That letter may then have come to be known as the Letter to the Ephesians, because it was in Ephesus that the only extant copy survived.

The second suggested explanation was propounded by Harnack, the great German scholar. In the later days the church in Laodicea sadly fell from grace. In the *Revelation* there is a letter to Laodicea which makes sad reading (*Revelation* 3: 14–22). In that letter the church of Laodicea is unsparingly condemned by the Risen Christ, so much so that he says to her in that vivid phrase: "I will spew you out of my mouth" (*Revelation* 3: 16). Now in the ancient world there was a custom called *damnatio memoriae*, the condemnation of a man's memory. A man might have rendered many a signal service to the state, for which his name might occur in books, in the state annals, in inscriptions and on memorials. But if such a man ended in some base act, some utter wreck of honour, his memory was condemned. His name was erased from all books, obliterated from all inscriptions, chiselled out of all memorials. Harnack thinks it possible that the church of Laodicea underwent a *damnatio memoriae* so that her very name was obliterated from the Christian records. If that were so, then the copies of the Letter to Laodicea would have no address at all; and when the collection was made at Ephesus, the name of Ephesus might well have become attached to it.

THE CIRCULAR LETTER

Both these suggestions are possible but still another suggestion is far more likely. We believe that *Ephesians was not in fact written to any one church, but was a circular letter to all Paul's Asian churches.* Let us look again at *Colossians* 4: 16. He writes: "And when this letter has been read among you, have it read also in the church at Laodicea; and see that you read also the letter from Laodicea." Paul does not say that the Colossians must read the epistle *to* Laodicea; they must read the epistle *from* Laodicea. It is as if Paul said: "There is a letter circulating; at the present moment it has reached Laodicea; when it is sent on to you from Laodicea be sure to read it." That sounds very like as if there was a letter circulating among the Asian churches, and we believe that letter was *Ephesians*.

THE QUINTESSENCE OF PAUL

If this be so, *Ephesians* is Paul's supreme letter. We have seen that *Ephesians* and *Colossians* are very close to each other. We believe that what happened was that Paul wrote *Colossians* to deal with a definite situation, an outbreak of heresy. In so doing he stumbled on his great expression of the all-sufficiency of Christ. He said to himself: "This is something that I must get across to all men." So he took the matter he had used in *Colossians,* removed all the local and temporary and controversial aspects, and wrote a new letter to tell all men of the all-sufficient Christ. *Ephesians*, as we see it, is the one letter Paul sent to all the eastern churches to tell them that the destined unity of all men and of all things could never be found except in Christ, and to tell them of the supreme task of the Church—that of being Christ's instrument in the universal reconciliation of man to man and of man to God. That is why *Ephesians* is the Queen of the Epistles.

EPHESIANS

IN *Ephesians* Paul's argument is very closely woven together. It often proceeds in long complicated sentences which are difficult to unravel. If we are really to grasp his meaning, there are passages where it will be better to read the letter, first in fairly long sections and then break down these sections into shorter passages for detailed study.

THE PURPOSE OF GOD

Ephesians 1: 1–14

This is a letter from Paul, an apostle of Jesus Christ, through the will of God, to God's consecrated people who live in Ephesus and who are faithful in Jesus Christ. Grace be to you and peace from God our Father and from the Lord Jesus Christ.

Blessed be the God and Father of our Lord Jesus Christ, who has blessed us with all the spiritual blessings which are only to be found in heaven, even as he chose us in him before the foundation of the world, that we might be holy and blameless before him. He determined in his love before time began to adopt us to himself through Jesus Christ, in the good purpose of his will, so that all might praise the glory of the generous gift which he freely gave us in the Beloved. For it is in him that we have a deliverance which cost his life; in him we have received the forgiveness of sins, which only the wealth of his grace could give, a grace which he gave us in abundant supply, and which conferred on us all wisdom and all sound sense. This happened because he made known to us the once hidden, but now revealed, secret of his will, for so it was his good pleasure to do. This secret was a purpose which he formed in his own mind before time began, so that the periods of time should be controlled and administered until they reached their full development, a development in which all things, in heaven and upon earth, are gathered into one in Jesus Christ. It was in Christ, in whom our portion in this scheme was also assigned to us, that it was determined, by the decision of him who controls everything according to the purpose of his will, that we, who were the first to set our hopes upon the coming of the Anointed One of God, should become the means whereby his glory should be praised. And it was in Christ that it was determined that you, too, should become the means whereby God's glory is praised, after you had heard the word which brings the truth, the good news of your salvation—that good news, in which, after you had come to believe, you were sealed with the Holy Spirit, who had been promised to you, the Spirit who is the foretaste and guarantee of all that one day we will inherit, until we enter into that complete redemption which brings complete possession.

GREETINGS TO GOD'S PEOPLE

Ephesians 1: 1, 2

This is a letter from Paul, an apostle of Jesus Christ, through the will of God, to God's consecrated people who live in Ephesus and who are faithful in Jesus Christ. Grace be to you, and peace from God our Father and from the Lord Jesus Christ.

PAUL begins his letter with the only two claims to fame which he possessed. (i) He is *an apostle of Christ.* When Paul said that there were three things in his mind. (*a*) He meant that he *belonged* to Christ. His life was not his own to do with as he liked; he was the possession of Jesus Christ, and he must always live as Jesus Christ wanted him to live. (*b*) He meant that he was sent out by Jesus Christ. The word *apostolos* comes from the verb *apostellein*, which means *to send out.* It can be used, for instance, of a naval squadron sent out on an expedition; it can be used of an ambassador sent out by his native country. It describes a man who is sent out with some special task to do. The Christian all through life sees himself as a member of the task force of Christ. He is a man with a mission, the mission of serving Christ within this world. (*c*) He meant that *any power he possessed was a delegated power.* The Sanhedrin was the supreme court of the Jews. In matters of religion the Sanhedrin had authority over every Jew throughout the world. When the Sanhedrin came to a decision, that decision was given to an *apostolos* to convey it to the persons whom it concerned and to see that it was

carried out. When such an *apostolos* went out, behind him
and in him lay the authority of the Sanhedrin, whose
representative he was. The Christian is the representative of
Christ within the world, but he is not left to carry out
that task in his own strength and power; the strength and
power of Jesus Christ are with him.

(ii) Paul goes on to say that he is an apostle *through the
will of God*. The accent in his voice here is not that of pride but
of sheer amazement. To the end of the day Paul was amazed
that God could have chosen a man like him to do his work.

> "How Thou canst think so well of us,
>   And be the God Thou art,
> Is darkness to my intellect,
>   But sunshine to my heart."

A Christian must never be filled with pride in any task that
God gives him to do; he must be filled with wonder that God
thought him worthy of a share in his work.

Paul goes on to address his letter to the people who live in
Ephesus and who are faithful in Jesus Christ. The Christian
is a man who always lives a double life. Paul's friends were
people who lived *in Ephesus* and *in Christ*. Every Christian
has a human address and a divine address; and that is precisely
the secret of the Christian life. Alister MacLean tells of a lady
in the West Highlands who lived a hard life, yet one of
perpetual serenity. When asked the secret of it, she answered:
"My secret is to sail the seas, and always to keep my heart
in port." Wherever the Christian is, he is still in Christ.

Paul begins with his usual greeting. "Grace to you," he says,
"and peace." Here are the two great words of the Christian
faith.

Grace has always two main ideas in it. The Greek word is
charis which could mean *charm*. There must be a certain
loveliness in the Christian life. A Christianity which is un-
attractive is no real Christianity. Grace always describes a gift,
and a gift which it would have been impossible for a man
to procure for himself, and which he never earned and in

no way deserved. Whenever we mention the word grace, we must think of the sheer loveliness of the Christian life and the sheer undeserved generosity of the heart of God.

When we think of the word *peace* in connection with the Christian life we must be careful. In Greek the word is *eirēnē*, but it translates the Hebrew word *shalōm*. In the Bible *peace* is never a purely negative word; it never describes simply the absence of trouble. *Shalōm* means everything which makes for a man's highest good. Christian peace is something quite independent of outward circumstances. A man might live in ease and luxury and on the fat of the land, he might have the finest of houses and the biggest of bank accounts, and yet not have peace; on the other hand, a man might be starving in prison, or dying at the stake, or living a life from which all comfort had fled, and be at perfect peace. The explanation is that there is only one source of peace in all the world, and that is doing the will of God. When we are doing something which we know we ought not to do or are evading something that we know we ought to do, there is always a haunting dispeace at the back of our minds; but if we are doing something very difficult, even something we do not want to do, so long as we know that it is the right thing there is a certain contentment in our hearts. "In his will is our peace."

THE CHOSEN OF GOD

Ephesians 1 : 3, 4

Blessed be the God and Father of our Lord Jesus Christ, who has blessed us with all the spiritual blessings which are only to be found in heaven, even as he chose us in him before the foundation of the world, that we might be holy and blameless before him.

IN the Greek the long passage from verse 3 to verse 14 is one sentence. It is so long and complicated because it represents not so much a reasoned statement as a lyrical song of praise. Paul's mind goes on and on, not because he is thinking in logical stages, but because gift after gift and wonder after wonder from God pass before his eyes. To understand it we must break it up and take it in short sections.

In this section Paul is thinking of the Christians as the chosen people of God, and his mind runs along three lines.

(i) He thinks of the *fact of God's choice*. Paul never thought of himself as having chosen to do God's work. He always thought of God as having chosen him. Jesus said to his disciples: "You did not choose me, but I chose you" (*John* 15: 16). Here precisely lies the wonder. It would not be so wonderful that man should choose God; the wonder is that God should choose man.

(ii) Paul thinks of *the bounty of God's choice*. God chose us to bless us with the blessings which are to be found only in heaven. There are certain things which a man can discover for himself; but there are others which are beyond his obtaining. A man by himself can acquire a certain skill, can achieve a certain position, can amass a certain amount of this world's goods; but by himself he can never attain to goodness or to peace of mind. God chose us to give us those things which he alone can give.

(iii) Paul thinks of *the purpose of God's choice*. God chose us that we should be *holy* and *blameless*. Here are two great words. *Holy* is the Greek word *hagios*, which always has in it the idea of *difference* and of *separation*. A temple is *holy* because it is different from other buildings; a priest is *holy* because he is different from ordinary men; a victim is *holy* because it is different from other animals; God is supremely *holy* because he is different from men; the Sabbath is *holy* because it is different from other days. So, then, God chose the Christian that he should be *different* from other men.

Here is the challenge that the modern Church has been very slow to face. In the early Church the Christian never had any doubt that he must be different from the world; he, in fact, knew that he must be so different that the probability was that the world would kill him and the certainty was that the world would hate him. But the tendency in the modern Church has been to play down the difference between the Church and the world. We have, in effect, often said to people: "So long as you live a decent, respectable life, it is quite all right to become a Church member and to call yourself a Christian. You don't need to be so very different from other people." In fact a Christian should be identifiable in the world.

It must always be remembered that this difference on which Christ insists is not one which takes a man *out* of the world; it makes him different *within* the world. It should be possible to identify the Christian in the school, the shop, the factory, the office, the hospital ward, everywhere. And the difference is that the Christian behaves not as any human laws compel him to do but as the law of Christ compels him to do. A Christian teacher is out to satisfy the regulations not of an education authority or a headmaster but of Christ; and that will almost certainly mean a very different attitude to the pupils under his charge. A Christian workman is out to satisfy the regulations not of a Trades Union but of Jesus Christ; and that will certainly make him a very different kind of workman, which may well end in him being so different that he is expelled from his union. A Christian doctor will never regard a sick person as a case, but always as a person. A Christian employer will be concerned with far more than the payment of minimum wages or the creation of minimum working conditions. It is the simple fact of the matter that if enough Christians became *hagios,* different, they would revolutionize society.

Blameless is the Greek word *amōmos.* Its interest lies in the fact that it is a sacrificial word. Under Jewish law before an animal could be offered as a sacrifice it must be inspected; and if any blemish was found it must be rejected as unfit for an offering to God. Only the best was fit to offer to God. *Amōmos* thinks of the whole man as an offering to God. It thinks of taking every part of our life, work, pleasure, sport, home life, personal relationships, and making them all such

that they can be offered to God. This word does not mean
that the Christian must be respectable; it means that he must
be perfect. To say that the Christian must be *amōmos* is to
banish contentment with second bests; it means that the
Christian standard is nothing less than perfection.

THE PLAN OF GOD

Ephesians 1: 5, 6

> He determined in his love before time began to adopt us to himself
> through Jesus Christ, in the good purpose of his will, so that all
> might praise the glory of the generous gift which he freely gave us
> in the Beloved.

IN this passage Paul speaks to us of the plan of God. One
of the pictures that he more than once uses of what God does
for men is that of adoption (cf. *Romans* 8: 23; *Galatians* 4: 5).
God adopted us as sons into his family.

In the ancient world, where Roman law prevailed, this
would be an even more meaningful picture than it is to us.
For there the family was based on what was called the *patria
potestas*, the father's power. A father had absolute power over
his children so long as he and they lived. He could sell his
child as a slave or even kill him. Dion Cassius tells us that
"the law of the Romans gives a father absolute authority
over his son, and that for the son's whole life. It gives him
authority, if he so chooses, to imprison him, to scourge him,
to make him work on his estate as a slave in fetters, even
to kill him. That right still continues to exist even if the son
is old enough to play an active part in political affairs,
even if he has been judged worthy to occupy the magistrate's
office, and even if he is held in honour by all men." It is
quite true that, when a father was judging his son, he was
supposed to call the adult male members of the family into
consultation, but it was not necessary that he should do so.

There are actual instances of a father condemning his son

to death. Sallust (*The Catiline Conspiracy*, 39) tells how Aulus Fulvius joined the rebel Catiline. He was arrested on the journey and brought back. And his father ordered that he should be put to death. The father did this on his own private authority, giving as his reason that "he had begotten him, not for Catiline against his country, but for his country against Catiline."

Under Roman law a child could not possess anything; and any inheritance willed to him, or any gift given to him, became the property of his father. It did not matter how old the son was, or to what honours and responsibility he had risen, he was absolutely in his father's power.

In circumstances like that it is obvious that adoption was a very serious step. It was, however, not uncommon, for children were often adopted to ensure that some family should not become extinct. The ritual of adoption must have been very impressive. It was carried out by a symbolic sale in which copper and scales were used. Twice the real father sold his son, and twice he symbolically bought him back; finally he sold him a third time, and at the third sale he did not buy him back. After this the adopting father had to go to the *praetor*, one of the principal Roman magistrates, and plead the case for the adoption. Only after all this had been gone through was the adoption complete.

When the adoption was complete it was complete indeed. The person who had been adopted had all the rights of a legitimate son in his new family and completely lost all rights in his old family. In the eyes of the law he was a new person. So new was he that even all debts and obligations connected with his previous family were abolished as if they had never existed.

That is what Paul says that God has done for us. We were absolutely in the power of sin and of the world; God, through Jesus, took us out of that power into his; and that adoption wipes out the past and makes us new.

THE GIFTS OF GOD

Ephesians 1: 7, 8

> For it is in him that we have a deliverance which cost his life;
> in him we have received the forgiveness of sins, which only the
> wealth of his grace could give, a grace which he gave us in abundant
> supply, and which conferred on us all wisdom and all sound sense.

IN this short section we come face to face with three of the
great conceptions of the Christian faith.

(i) There is *deliverance*. The word used is *apolutrōsis*. It
comes from the verb *lutroun*, which means to *ransom*. It is
the word used for ransoming a man who is a prisoner of
war or a slave; for freeing a man from the penalty of death;
for God's deliverance of the children of Israel from their
slavery in Egypt; for God's continual rescuing of his people
in the time of their trouble. In every case the conception
is the delivering of a man from a situation from which he
was powerless to liberate himself or from a penalty which he
himself could never have paid.

So, then, first of all Paul says that God delivered men from
a situation from which they could never have delivered themselves. That is precisely what Christianity did do for men.
When Christianity came into this world men were haunted
by the sense of their own powerlessness. They knew the
wrongness of the life which they were living; and also that
they were powerless to do anything about it.

Seneca is full of this kind of feeling of helpless frustration.
Men, he said, were overwhelmingly conscious of their in-
efficiency in necessary things. He said of himself that he was a
homo non tolerabilis, a man not to be tolerated. Men, he said
with a kind of despair, love their vices and hate them at the
same time. What men need, he cried, is a hand let down
to lift them up. The highest thinkers in the pagan world knew
that they were in the grip of something from which they were
helpless to deliver themselves. They needed liberation.

It was just that liberation which Jesus Christ brought. It is still true that he can liberate men from helpless slavery to the things which attract and disgust them at one and the same time. To put it at its simplest, Jesus can still make bad men good.

(ii) There is *forgiveness*. The ancient world was haunted by the sense of sin. It might well be said that the whole Old Testament is an expansion of the saying, "The soul that sins shall die" (*Ezekiel* 18: 4). Men were conscious of their own guilt and stood in terror of their god or gods. It is sometimes said that the Greeks had no sense of sin. Nothing could be further from the truth. "Men," said Hesiod, "delight their souls in cherishing that which is their bane." All the plays of Aeschylus are founded on one text—"The doer shall suffer." Once a man had done an evil thing Nemesis was on his heels; and punishment followed sin as certainly as night followed day. As Shakespeare had it in *Richard the Third*,

> "My conscience hath a thousand several tongues,
> And every tongue brings in a several tale,
> And every tale condemns me for a villain."

If there was one thing which men knew it was the sense of sin and the dread of God. Jesus changed all that. He taught men, not of the hate, but of the love of God. Because Jesus came into the world, men, even in their sin, discovered God's love.

(iii) There is *wisdom* and *sound sense*. The two words in Greek are *sophia* and *phronēsis*, and Christ brought both of them to us. This is very interesting. The Greeks wrote much about these two words; if a man had both, he was perfectly equipped for life.

Aristotle defined *sophia* as knowledge of the most precious things. Cicero defined it as knowledge of things both human and divine. *Sophia* was a thing of the searching intellect. *Sophia* was the answer to the eternal problems of life and death, and God and man, and time and eternity.

Aristotle defined *phronēsis* as the knowledge of human affairs and of the things in which planning is necessary.

Plutarch defined it as practical knowledge of the things which concern us. Cicero defined it as knowledge of the things which are to be sought and the things which are to be avoided. Plato defined it as the disposition of mind which enables us to judge what things are to be done and what things are not to be done. In other words, *phronēsis* is the sound sense which enables men to meet and to solve the practical problems of everyday life and living.

It is Paul's claim that Jesus brought us *sophia*, the intellectual knowledge which satisfies the mind, and *phronēsis,* the practical knowledge which enables us to handle the day to day problems of practical life and living. There is a certain completeness in the Christian character. There is a type of person who is at home in the study, who moves familiarly amidst the theological and philosophical problems, and who is yet helpless and impractical in the ordinary everyday affairs of life. There is another kind of person who claims that he is a practical man, so engaged with the business of living that he has no time to concern himself with the ultimate things. In the light of the gifts of God through Christ, both of these characters are imperfect. Christ brings to us the solution of the problems both of eternity and time.

THE GOAL OF HISTORY

Ephesians 1: 9, 10

> This happened because he made known to us the once hidden but now revealed secret of his will, for so it was his good pleasure to do. The secret was a purpose which he formed in his own mind before time began, so that the periods of time should be controlled and administered until they reached their full development, a development in which all things, in heaven and upon earth, are gathered into one in Jesus Christ.

IT is now that Paul is really getting to grips with his subject. He says, as the Authorized Version has it, that God has made known to us "the mystery of his will." The New

Testament uses the word *mystery* in a special sense. It is not something mysterious in the sense that it is hard to understand. It is something which has long been kept secret and has now been revealed, but is still incomprehensible to the person who has not been initiated into its meaning.

Let us take an example. Suppose someone who knew nothing whatever about Christianity was brought into a Communion service. To him it would be a complete mystery; he would not understand in the least what was going on. But to a man who knows the story and the meaning of the Last Supper, the whole service has a meaning which is quite clear. So in the New Testament sense a mystery is something which is hidden to the heathen but clear to the Christian.

What for Paul was the mystery of the will of God? It was that the gospel was open to the Gentiles too. In Jesus God has revealed that his love and care, his grace and mercy, are meant, not only for the Jews, but for all the world.

Now Paul, in one sentence, drops his great thought. Up till now men had been living in a divided world. There was division between the beasts and men. There was division between the Jew and the Gentile, the Greek and the barbarian. All over the world there was strife and tension. Jesus came into the world to wipe out the divisions. That for Paul was the secret of God. It was God's purpose that all the many different strands and all the warring elements in this world should be gathered into one in Jesus Christ.

Here we have another tremendous thought. Paul says that all history has been a working out of this process. He says that through all the ages there has been an arranging and an administering of things that this day of unity should come. The word which Paul uses for this preparation is intensely interesting. It is *oikonomia*, which literally means *household management*. The *oikonomos* was the steward who saw to it that the family affairs ran smoothly.

It is the Christian conviction that history is the working out of the will of God. That is by no means what every historian or thinker has been able to see. Oscar Wilde in one of his epigrams said: "You give the criminal calendar of Europe to your children under the name of history." G. N. Clark, in his inaugural lecture at Cambridge, said: "There is no secret and no plan in history to be discovered. I do not believe that any future consummation could make sense of all the irrationalities of preceding ages. If it could not explain them, still less could it justify them." In the introduction to *A History of Europe*, H. A. L. Fisher writes: "One intellectual excitement, however, has been denied to me. Men wiser and more learned than I have discovered in history a plot, a rhythm, a predetermined pattern. These harmonies are concealed from me. I can see only one emergency following another, as wave follows upon wave, only one great fact with respect to which, since it is unique, there can be no generalizations, only one safe rule for the historian: that he should recognize in the development of human destinies the play of the contingent and the unforeseen." Andre Maurois says: "The universe is indifferent. Who created it? Why are we here on this puny mud-heap spinning in infinite space? I have not the slightest idea, and I am quite convinced that no one has the least idea."

It so happens that we are living in an age in which men have lost their faith in any purpose for this world. But it is the faith of the Christian that in this world God's purpose is being worked out; and it is the conviction of Paul that that purpose is that one day all things and all men should be one family in Christ. As Paul sees it, that mystery was not even grasped until Jesus came and now it is the great task of the Church to work out God's purpose of unity, revealed in Jesus Christ.

JEW AND GENTILE

Ephesians 1: 11–14

It was in Christ, in whom our portion in this scheme was also assigned to us, that it was determined, by the decision of him who controls everything according to the purpose of his good will, that we, who were the first to set our hopes upon the coming of the Anointed One of God, should become the means whereby his glory should be praised. And it was in Christ that it was determined that you too should become the means whereby God's glory is praised, after you had heard the word which brings the truth, the good news of your salvation—that good news in which after you had believed you were sealed with the Holy Spirit, who had been promised to you, the Spirit who is the foretaste and guarantee of all that one day we will inherit, until we enter into that complete redemption which brings complete possession.

HERE is Paul's first example of the new unity which Christ brings. When he speaks of *us* he means his own nation, the Jews; when he speaks of *you* he means the Gentiles to whom he is writing; and when in the very last sentence he uses *we*, it is of Jews and Gentiles together that he is thinking.

First of all, Paul speaks of the Jews. They, too, had their portion assigned to them in the plan of God. They were the first to believe in the coming of the Anointed One of God. All through their history they had dreamed of and expected the Messiah. Their part in the scheme of things was to be the nation from whom God's chosen one should come.

Adam Smith, the great economist, argued that the whole pattern of life was founded on what he called *the division of labour*. He meant that life can only go on when each man has a job and does that job, and when the results of all the jobs are pooled and become the common stock. The shoemaker makes shoes; the baker makes bread; the tailor makes clothes; each has his own job, and each sticks to his own job; and when each efficiently carries out his job the total good of the whole community follows.

What is true of individuals is true also of nations. Each nation has its part in God's scheme of things. The Greeks taught men what beauty of thought and form is. The Romans taught men law and the science of government and administration. The Jews taught men religion. The Jews were the people who were so prepared that from them God's Messiah should come.

That is not to say that God did not prepare other people too. All over the world God had been preparing men and nations so that their mind would be ready to receive the message of Christianity when it came. But the great privilege of the Jewish nation was that they were the first to expect the coming of the Anointed One of God into the world.

Then Paul turns to the Gentiles. In their development he sees two stages.

(i) They received the word; to them the Christian preachers brought the Christian message. That word was two things. First, it was the word of truth; it brought them the truth about God and about the world in which they lived and about themselves. Second, it was good news; it was the message of the love and of the grace of God.

(ii) They were sealed with the Holy Spirit. In the ancient world—it is a custom still followed—when a sack, or a crate, or a package was despatched, it was sealed with a seal, in order to indicate from where it had come and to whom it belonged. The possession of the Holy Spirit is the seal which shows that a man belongs to God. The Holy Spirit both shows us God's will and enables us to do it.

Here Paul says a great thing about the Holy Spirit. He calls the Holy Spirit, as the Authorized Version has it, *the earnest of our redemption*. The Greek word is *arrabōn*. The *arrabōn* was a regular feature of the Greek business world. It was a part of the purchase price of anything, paid in advance as a guarantee that the rest would in due time be paid. There are many Greek commercial documents still extant in which the word occurs. A woman sells a cow and receives so many drachmae as *arrabōn*. Some dancing girls are engaged for a public entertainment and are paid so much in advance. What Paul is saying is that the experience of the Holy Spirit which we have in this world is a foretaste of the blessedness of heaven; and it is the guarantee that some day we will enter into full possession of the blessedness of God.

The highest experiences of Christian peace and joy which

this world can afford are only faint foretastes of the joy into which we will one day enter. It is as if God had given us enough to whet our appetites for more and enough to make us certain that some day he will give us all.

THE MARKS OF THE CHURCH

Ephesians 1: 15–23

> It is because I have heard of your faith in Jesus Christ, and your love to all God's consecrated people, that I never cease to give thanks for you, as I remember you in my prayers. It is the aim of my prayers that the God of our Lord Jesus Christ, the glorious Father, may give you the Spirit of wisdom, the Spirit which brings you new revelation, as you come to know him more and more fully. It is the aim of my prayers that the eyes of your heart may be enlightened, so that you may know what hope his calling has brought to you, what wealth of glory there is in our inheritance among the saints, what surpassing greatness there is in his power to us who believe with a belief which was wrought by the might of his strength, that power which wrought in Christ to raise him from among the dead, and to set him at God's right hand in the heavenly places, above every rule and authority and power and lordship, above every dignity which is held in honour, not only in this age, but also in the age to come. God subjected all things to him, and he gave him as head above all to the Church, which is his body, the Church which is his complement on earth, the Church which belongs to him who is filling all things in all places.

THE supremely important part, the second great step in Paul's argument, lies at the very end of this passage; but there are certain things we must note in the verses which go before.

Here there is set out before us in a perfect summary the characteristics of a true Church. Paul has heard of their faith in Christ and their love to all God's consecrated people. The two things which must characterize any true Church are *loyalty to Christ* and *love to men*.

There is a loyalty to Christ which does not issue in love to men. The monks and the hermits had a loyalty to Christ which made them abandon the ordinary activities of life in order to live alone in the desert places. The heresy hunters of the Spanish Inquisition and of many another age had a loyalty to Christ which made them persecute those who thought differently from them. Before Jesus came the Pharisees had a loyalty to God which made them contemptuous of those whom they thought less loyal than themselves.

The true Christian loves Christ and loves his fellow men. More than that, he knows that he cannot show his love to Christ in any other way than by showing his love to his fellow men. However orthodox a Church is, however pure its theology, and however noble its worship and its liturgy, it is not a true Church in the real sense of the term unless it is characterized by love for its fellow men. There are Churches which seldom make any public pronouncement which is not based on censorious criticism. They may be orthodox, but they are not Christian. The true Church is marked by a double love—love for Christ and love for men.

F. W. Boreham quotes a passage from Robert Buchanan's *Shadow of the Sword*, in which Buchanan describes the Chapel of Hate. "It stood on a bleak and barren moor in Brittany a hundred years ago. It was in ruins; the walls were black and stained with the slime of centuries; around the crumbling altar nettles and rank weeds grew breast high; whilst black mists, charged with rain, brooded night and day about the gloomy scene. Over the doorway of the chapel, but half-obliterated, was its name. It was dedicated to Our Lady of Hate. 'Hither,' says Buchanan, 'in hours of passion and pain, came men and women to cry curses on their enemies—the maiden on her false lover, the lover on his false mistress, the husband on his false wife—praying, one and all, that Our Lady of Hate might hearken, and that the hated one might die within the year.'" And then the novelist adds: "So bright and so deep had the gentle Christian light shone within their minds!"

A chapel of hate is a grim conception; and yet—are we always so very far away from it? We hate the liberals or the radicals; we hate the fundamentalists or the obscurantists; we hate the man whose theology is different from our own; we hate the Roman Catholic or the the Protestant as the case may be. We make pronouncements which are characterized, not by Christian charity, but by a kind of condemning bitterness. We would do well to remember every now and then that love of Christ and love of our fellow men cànnot exist without each other. Our tragedy is that it is so often true, as Swift once said: "We have just enough religion to make us hate, but not enough to make us love one another."

PAUL'S PRAYER FOR THE CHURCH

Ephesians 1: 15–23 (*continued*)

IN this passage we see what Paul asks for a Church which he loves and which is doing well.

(i) He prays for the Spirit of Wisdom. The word he uses for *wisdom* is *sophia*, and we have already seen that *sophia* is the wisdom of the deep things of God. He prays that the Church may be led deeper and deeper into the knowledge of the eternal truths. If ever that is to happen, certain things are necessary.

(*a*) It is necessary that we should have a thinking people. Boswell tells us that Goldsmith once said: "As I take my shoes from the shoemaker, and my coat from the tailor, so I take my religion from the priest." There are many who are like that; and yet religion is nothing unless it is a personal discovery. As Plato had it long ago: "The unexamined life is the life not worth living," and the unexamined religion is the religion not worth having. It is an obligation for a thinking man to think his way to God.

(*b*) It is necessary that we should have a teaching ministry. William Chillingworth said: "The Bible, and the Bible only, is the religion of Protestants." That is true; but so often we would not think so. The exposition of scripture from the pulpit is a first necessity of religious wakening.

(*c*) It is necessary that we should have a readjusted sense of proportion. It is one of the strange facts of Church life that in Church courts, such as sessions and presbyteries, and even General Assemblies, a score of hours might be given to the discussion of mundane problems of administration for every one given to the discussion of the eternal verities of God.

(ii) Paul prays for a fuller revelation and a fuller knowledge of God. For the Christian growth in knowledge and in grace is essential. Any man who follows a profession knows that he dare not stop studying. No doctor thinks that he has finished learning when he leaves the classrooms of his university. He knows that week by week, and almost day by day, new techniques and treatments are being discovered; and if he wishes to continue to be of service to those in illness and in pain, he must keep up with them. It is so with the Christian. The Christian life could be described as getting to know God better every day. A friendship which does not grow closer with the years tends to vanish with the years. And it is so with us and God.

(iii) He prays for a new realization of the Christian hope. It is almost a characteristic of the age in which we live that it is an age of despair. Thomas Hardy wrote in Tess: "Sometimes I think that the worlds are like apples on our stubbard tree. Some of them splendid and some of them blighted." Then comes the question: "On which kind do we live—a splendid one or a blighted one?" And Tess's answer is: "A blighted one." Between the wars Sir Philip Gibbs wrote: "If I smell poison gas in Edgeware Road, I am not going to put on a gas mask or go to a gas-proof room. I am going out to take a good sniff of it, for I shall know that *the game is up*." H. G. Wells once wrote grimly: "Man, who began in a cave behind a windbreak, will end in the disease-soaked ruins of a slum." On every side the voice of the pessimist sounds; it was never more necessary to sound the trumpet-call of Christian hope. If the Christian message is true, the world is on the way not to dissolution but to consummation.

(iv) He prays for a new realization of the power of God.

For Paul the supreme proof of that power was the resurrection. It proved that God's purpose cannot be stopped by any action of men. In a world which looks chaotic, it is well to realize that God is still in control.

(v) Paul finishes by speaking of the conquest of Christ in a sphere which does not mean so much to us to-day. As the Authorized Version has it, God has raised Jesus Christ "far above all principality, and power, and might, and dominion, and every name that is named." In Paul's day men strongly believed both in demons and in angels; and these words which Paul uses are the titles of different grades of angels. He is saying that there is not a being in heaven or on earth to whom Jesus Christ is not superior. In essence Paul's prayer is that men should realize the greatness of the Saviour God has given to them.

THE BODY OF CHRIST

Ephesians 1: 15–23 (*continued*)

WE come to the last two verses of this chapter, and in them Paul has one of the most adventurous and most uplifting thoughts that any man has ever had. He calls the Church by its greatest title—*the body of Christ*.

In order to understand what Paul means, let us go back to the basic thought of his letter. As it stands, this world is a complete disunity. There is disunity between Jew and Gentile, between Greek and barbarian; there is disunity between different men within the same nation; there is disunity within every man, for in every man the good strives with the evil; there is disunity between man and the beasts; and, above all, there is disunity between man and God. It was Paul's thesis that Jesus died to bring all the discordant elements in this universe into one, to wipe out the separations, to reconcile man to man and to reconcile man to God. Jesus Christ was above all things God's instrument of reconciliation.

It was to bring all things and all men into one family that Christ died. But, clearly, that unity does not as yet exist. Let us take a human analogy. Suppose a great doctor discovers a cure for cancer. Once that cure is found it is there. But before it can become available for everyone, it must be taken out to the world. Doctors and surgeons must know about it and be trained to use it. The cure is there but one man cannot take it out to all the world; a corps of doctors must be the agents whereby it arrives at all the world's sufferers. That precisely is what the Church is to Jesus Christ. It is in Jesus that all men and all nations can become one; but before that can happen they must know about Jesus Christ. And it is the task of the Church to bring that about.

Christ is the head; the Church is the body. The head must have a body through which it can work. The Church is quite literally hands to do Christ's work, feet to run upon his errands, a voice to speak his words.

In the very last phrase of the chapter Paul has two tremendous thoughts. The Church, he says, is the complement of Christ. Just as the ideas of the mind cannot become effective without the work of the body, the tremendous glory which Christ brought to this world cannot be made effective without the work of the Church. Paul goes on to say that Jesus is bit by bit filling all things in all places; and that filling is being worked out by the Church. This is one of the most tremendous thoughts in all Christianity. It means nothing less than that God's plan for one world is in the hands of the Church.

An illustration which is old and hackneyed perfectly sums up this great truth. There is a legend which tells how Jesus went back to heaven after his time on earth. Even in heaven he bore upon him the marks of the Cross. The angels were talking to him and Gabriel said: "Master, you must have suffered terribly for men down there." "I did," said Jesus. "And," said Gabriel, "do they all know about how you loved them and what you did for them?" "O no," said Jesus, "not yet. Just now only a few people in Palestine know." "What have you done," said Gabriel, "to let everyone know about it?" Jesus said: "I have asked Peter and James and

John and a few others to make it the business of their lives to tell others about me, and the others still others, and yet others, until the farthest man on the widest circle knows what I have done." Gabriel looked very doubtful, for he knew well what poor stuff men were made of. "Yes," he said, "but what if Peter and James and John grow tired? What if the people who come after them forget? What if away down in the twentieth century people just don't tell others about you? Haven't you made any other plans?" And Jesus answered: "I haven't made any other plans. *I'm counting on them.*" To say that the Church is the Body means that Jesus is counting on us.

THE CHRISTLESS LIFE AND THE GRACE OF GOD

Ephesians 2: 1–10

When you were dead in your sins and trespasses, those sins and trespasses in which once you walked, living life in the way in which this present age of this world lives it, living life as the ruler of the power of the air dictates it, that spirit who now operates in the children of disobedience—and once all we too lived the same kind of life as these children of disobedience do, a life in which we were at the mercy of the desires of our lower nature, a life in which we followed the wishes of our lower nature and of our own designs, a life in which, so far as human nature goes, we deserved nothing but the wrath of God, as the others do—although we were all like that, I say, God, because he is rich in mercy, and because of his great love with which he has loved us, made us alive in Christ Jesus, even when we were dead in trespasses (it is by grace you have been saved), and raised us up with Christ, and gave us a seat in the heavenly places with Christ, because of what Christ Jesus did for us. This he did so that in the age to come the surpassing riches of his grace in his kindness to us in Christ Jesus might be demonstrated. For it is by grace appropriated by faith that you have been saved. You had nothing to do with this. It was God's gift to you. It was not the result of works, for it was God's design that no one should be able to boast. For we are his work, created in Christ Jesus for good works, works which God prepared beforehand that we might walk in them.

IN this passage Paul's thought flows on regardless of the rules of grammar; he begins sentences and never finishes them; he begins with one construction and halfway through he glides into another. That is because this is far more a lyric of the love of God than a careful theological exposition. The song of the nightingale is not to be analysed by the laws of musical composition. The lark sings for the joy of singing. That is what Paul is doing here. He is pouring out his heart, and the claims of grammar have to give way to the wonder of grace.

LIFE WITHOUT CHRIST

Ephesians 2: 1–3

> When you were dead in your sins and trespasses, those sins and trespasses in which you once walked, living life in the way this present age lives it, living life as the ruler of the power of the air dictates it, that spirit who now operates in the children of disobedience—and once all we too lived the same kind of life as these children of disobedience do, a life in which we were at the mercy of the desires of our lower nature, a life in which we followed the wishes of our lower nature and of our own designs, a life in which, as far as human nature goes, we deserved nothing but the wrath of God, as the others do.

WHEN Paul speaks of *you*, he is speaking of the Gentiles; when he speaks of *us* he is speaking of the Jews, his fellow countrymen. In this passage he shows how terrible the Christless life was for Gentile and for Jew alike.

(i) He says that that life was lived in sins and trespasses. The words he uses are interesting. The word for *sin* is *hamartia*; and *hamartia* is a shooting word. It literally means a *miss*. A man shoots his arrow at the target; the arrow misses; that is *hamartia*. Sin is the failure to hit the target of life. That is precisely why sin is so universal.

We commonly have a wrong idea of sin. We would readily agree that the robber, murderer, the razor-slasher, the drunkard, the gangster are sinners; but, since most of us are respectable citizens, in our heart of hearts we think that sin has not very much to do with us. We would probably rather resent being called hell-deserving sinners. But *hamartia* brings us face to face with what sin is, the failure to be what we ought to be and could be.

Is a man as good a husband as he might be? Does he try to make life easier for his wife? Does he inflict his moods on his family? Is a woman as good a wife as she might be? Does she really take an interest in her husband's work and try to understand his problems and his worries? Are we as good parents as we might be? Do we discipline and train our children as we ought, or do we often shirk the issue? As our children grow older, do we come nearer to them, or do they drift away until conversation is often difficult and we and they are practically strangers? Are we as good sons and daughters as we might be? Do we ever even try to say thank you for what has been done for us? Do we ever see the hurt look in our parents' eyes and know that we put it there? Are we as good workmen as we could be? Is every working hour filled with our most conscientious work and is every task done as well as we could possibly do it?

When we realize what sin is, we come to see that it is not something which theologians have invented. It is something with which life is permeated. It is the failure in any sphere of life to be what we ought to be and could be.

The other word Paul uses, translated *trespasses* is *paraptōma*. This literally means *a slip* or *a fall*. It is used for a man losing the way and straying from the right road; it is used for a man failing to grasp and slipping away from the truth. Trespass, is taking the wrong road when we could take the right one; it is missing the truth that we should have known. Therefore it is the failure to reach the goal we ought to have reached.

Are we in life where we ought to be? Have we reached the goal of efficiency and skill that our gifts might have enabled us to reach? Have we reached the goal of service to others that we might have reached? Have we reached the goal of goodness to which we might have attained?

The central idea of sin is failure, failure to hit the target, failure to hold to the road, failure to make life what it was capable of becoming; and that definition includes every one of us.

DEATH IN LIFE

Ephesians 2: 1–3 (*continued*)

PAUL speaks about people being *dead in sins*. What did he mean? Some have taken it to mean that without Christ men live in a state of sin which in the life to come produces the death of the soul. But Paul is not talking about the life to come; he is talking about this present life. There are three directions in which the effect of sin is deadly.

(i) *Sin kills innocence*. No one is precisely the same after he has sinned. The psychologists tell us that we never forget anything.

It may not be in our conscious memory, but everything we ever did or saw or heard is buried in our subconscious memories. The result is that sin leaves a permanent effect on a man.

In Du Maurier's novel *Trilby* there is an example of that. For the first time in his life Little Billee has taken part in a drunken debauch and has himself been drunk. "And when, after some forty-eight hours or so, he had quite slept off the fumes of that memorable Christmas debauch, he found that a sad thing had happened to him, and a strange! It was as though a tarnishing breath had swept over the reminiscent mirror of his mind and left a little film behind it, so that no past thing he wished to see therein was reflected with quite the same pristine clearness. As though the keen, quick, razor edge of his power to reach and re-evoke the by-gone charm and glamour and essence of things had been blunted and coarsened. As though the bloom of that special joy, the gift he had of recalling past emotions and sensations and situations, and making them actual once more by a mere effort of will, had been brushed away. And he never recovered the full use of that most precious faculty, the boon of youth and happy childhood, and which he had once possessed, without knowing it, in such singular and exceptional completeness."

The experience of sin had left a kind of tarnishing film on his mind and things could never be quite the same again. If we stain a garment or a carpet, we may send it to be cleaned, but it is never again quite the same. Sin does something to a man; it kills innocence; and innocence, once lost, can never be recovered.

(ii) *Sin kills ideals.* In the lives of so many there is a kind of tragic process. At first a man regards some wrong thing with horror; the second stage comes when he is tempted into doing it, but even as he does it, he is still unhappy and ill at ease and very conscious that it is wrong; the third stage is when he has done the thing so often that he does it without a qualm. Each sin makes the next sin easier. Wordsworth in the *Intimations of Immortality* wrote:

> "The youth, who daily from the east
> Must travel, still is Nature's priest,
> 　And by the vision splendid
> 　Is on his way attended;
> At length the man perceives it die away,
> And fade into the light of common day."

Sin is a kind of suicide, for it kills the ideals which make life worth while.

(iii) In the end *sin kills the will.* At first a man engages in some forbidden pleasure because he wants to do so; in the end he engages in it because he cannot help doing so. Once a thing becomes a habit it is not far from being a necessity. When a man has allowed some habit, some indulgence, some forbidden practice to master him, he becomes its slave. As the old saying has it, "Sow an act and reap a habit; sow a habit and reap a character; sow a character and reap a destiny."

There is a certain murderous power in sin. It kills innocence; sin may be forgiven but its effect remains. As Origen had it: "The scars remain." Sin kills ideals; men begin to do without a qualm the thing which once they regarded with horror.

Sin kills the will; the thing so grips a man that he cannot break free.

THE MARKS OF THE CHRISTLESS LIFE

Ephesians 2: 1–3 (*continued*)

IN this passage Paul makes a kind of list of the characteristics of life without Christ.

(i) It is life lived in the way this present age lives it. That is to say, it is life lived on the world's standards and with the world's values. Christianity demands *forgiveness*, but the ancient writers said it was a sign of weakness to have the power to avenge oneself for injury and not to do so. Christianity demands *love* even to our enemies, but Plutarch said that the sign of a good man was that he was useful to his friends and terrible to his enemies. Christianity demands *service*, but the world cannot understand the missionary for instance, who goes away to some foreign land to teach in a school or heal in a hospital for a quarter of the salary he or she might obtain at home in some secular service. The essence of the world's standard is that it sets self in the centre; the essence of the Christian standard is that it sets Christ and others in the centre. The essence of the wordly man is, as someone has said, that "he knows the price of everything and the value of nothing." The world's motive is profit; the Christian's dynamic is the desire to serve.

(ii) It is life lived under the dictates of the prince of the air. Here again we are at something which was very real in the days of Paul but which is not so real to us. The ancient world believed strenuously in demons. They believed that the air was so crowded with these demons that there was not room to insert a pinpoint between them. Pythagoras said: "The whole air is full of Spirits." Philo said: "There are spirits flying everywhere through the air." "The air is the house of the disembodied spirits." These demons were not all bad, but many were, out to propagate evil, to frustrate the purposes of God and to ruin the souls of men. The man who is under their domination has taken sides against God.

(iii) It is a life characterized by disobedience. God has many ways of revealing his will to men. He does so by conscience, the voice of the Holy Spirit speaking within us; he does so by giving to men the wisdom and the commandments of his book; he does so through the advice of good and godly men. But the man who lives the Christless life takes his own way of things, even when he knows what God's way is.

(iv) It is a life which is at the mercy of desire. The word for desire is *epithumia* which characteristically means desire for the wrong and the forbidden thing. To succumb to that is inevitably to come to disaster.

One of the tragedies of the nineteenth century was the career of Oscar Wilde. He had a brilliant mind, and won the highest academic honours; he was a scintillating writer, and won the highest rewards in literature; he had all the charm in the world and was a man whose instinct it was to be kind; yet he fell to temptation and came to prison and disgrace. When he was suffering for his fall, he wrote his book *De Profundis* and in it he said: "The gods had given me almost everything. But I let myself be lured into long spells of senseless and sensual ease. . . . Tired of being on the heights I deliberately went to the depths in search for new sensation. What the paradox was to me in the sphere of thought, perversity became to me in the sphere of passion. I grew careless of the lives of others. I took pleasure where it pleased me, and passed on. I forgot that every little action of the common day makes or unmakes character, and that therefore what one has done in the secret chamber, one has some day to cry aloud from the house-top. I ceased to be lord over myself. I was no longer the captain of my soul, and did not know it. I allowed pleasure to dominate me. I ended in horrible disgrace."

Desire is a bad master, and to be at the mercy of desire is to be a slave. And desire is not simply a fleshly thing; it is the craving for any forbidden thing.

(v) It is the life which follows what the Authorized Version calls the desires of our flesh. We must be careful to understand what Paul means by the sins of the flesh. He means far more than sexual sins. In *Galatians* 5: 19–21 Paul lists the sins of the flesh. True, he starts with adultery and fornication, but he goes on to idolatry, hatred, wrath, strife, envyings, seditions, heresies. The flesh is that part of our nature which gives sin a bridgehead and a point of attack.

The meaning of "the flesh" will vary from person to person. One man's weakness may be in his body and his risk may be sexual sin; another's may be in spiritual things and his risk in pride; another's may be in earthly things and his risk unworthy ambition; another's sin may be in his temper and his risk in envyings and strife. All these are sins of the flesh. Let no man think that, because he has escaped the grosser sins of the body, he has avoided the sins of the flesh. The flesh is anything in us which gives sin its chance; it is human nature without God. To live according to the dictates of the flesh is simply to live in such a way that our lower nature, the worse part of us, dominates our lives.

(vi) It is life which is deserving only of the wrath of God. Many a man's life is embittered because he feels that he has never had what his talents and his work deserve; but in the sight of God no man deserves anything but condemnation. It is only his love in Christ which has forgiven men who deserved nothing but punishment from him, men who had grieved his love and broken his law.

THE WORK OF CHRIST

Ephesians 2: 4–10

Although we were all like that, I say, God, because he is rich in mercy and because of his great love with which he has loved us, made us alive in Jesus Christ, even when we were dead in trespasses (it is by grace you have been saved), and raised us up with Christ, and gave us a seat in the heavenly places with Christ, because of what Christ Jesus did for us. This he did so that in the age to come the surpassing riches of his grace in his kindness to us in Christ Jesus might be demonstrated. For it is by grace appropriated by faith that you have been saved. You had nothing to do with this. It was God's gift to you. It was not the result of works, for it was God's design that no one should be able to boast. For we are his work, created in Christ Jesus for good works, works which God prepared beforehand that we might walk in them.

PAUL had begun by saying that, as we are, we are dead in sins and trespasses; now he says that God in his love and mercy has made us alive in Jesus Christ. What exactly did he mean by that? We saw that there were three things involved in being dead in sins and trespasses. Jesus has something to do about each of them.

(i) We saw that sin kills innocence. Not even Jesus can give a man back his lost innocence, for not even Jesus can put back the clock; but what he can do is take away the sense of guilt which the lost innocence necessarily brings with it.

The first thing sin does is create a feeling of estrangement between us and God. Whenever a man realizes that he has sinned, he is oppressed with the feeling that he dare not approach God. When Isaiah received his vision of God, his first reaction was to say: "Woe is me! for I am lost; for I am a man of unclean lips, and I dwell in the midst of a people of unclean lips" (*Isaiah* 6: 5). When Peter realized who Jesus was, his first reaction was: "Depart from me, for I am a sinful man, O Lord" (*Luke* 5: 8).

Jesus begins by taking that sense of estrangement away. He came to tell us that no matter what we are like the door is open to the presence of God. Suppose there was a son who did some shameful thing and then ran away, because he was sure that there was no use in going home, because the door was bound to be shut. Then suppose someone came with the news that the door was still open and a welcome was waiting at home. What a difference that news would make! It was just that kind of news that Jesus brought.

He came to take away the sense of estrangement and of guilt, by telling us that God wants us just as we are.

(ii) We saw that sin killed the ideals by which men live. Jesus reawakens the ideal in the heart of man.

The story is told of a negro engineer in a river ferry-boat in America. His boat was old and he did not worry over much about it; the engines were begrimed and ill-cared for. This engineer was soundly converted. The first thing he did was to go back to his ferry-boat and polish his engines until every part of the machinery shone like a mirror. One of the regular passengers commented on the change. "What have you been up to?" he asked the engineer. "What set you cleaning and polishing these old engines of yours?" "Sir," answered the engineer, "I've got a glory." That is what Christ does for a man. He gives him a glory.

It is told that in the congregation in Edinburgh to which George Matheson came there was an old woman who lived in a cellar in filthy conditions. After some months of Matheson's ministry, communion time came round. When the elder called at this old woman's cellar with the cards, he found that she had gone. He tracked her down. He found her in an attic room. She was very poor and there were no luxuries, but the attic was as light and airy and clean as the cellar had been dark and dismal and dirty. "I see you've changed your house," he said to her. "Ay," she said, "I have. You canna hear George Matheson preach and live in a cellar." The Christian message had rekindled the ideal.

As the old hymn has it:

"Deep in the human heart, crushed by the tempter,
Feelings lie buried that grace can restore."

The grace of Jesus Christ rekindles the ideals which repeated falling to sin has extinguished. And by that very rekindling, life is set climbing again.

(iii) Greater than anything else, Jesus Christ revives and restores the lost will. We saw that the deadly thing about sin was that it slowly but surely destroyed a man's will and that the indulgence which had begun as a pleasure became a necessity. Jesus recreates the will.

That in fact is always what love does. The effect of a great love is always a cleansing thing. When a person really and truly falls in love, his love compels him to goodness. He loves the loved one so much that the love of his sins is broken.

That is what Christ does for us. When we love him, that love recreates and restores our will towards goodness. As the hymn has it:

> "He breaks the power of cancelled sin,
> He sets the prisoner free."

THE WORK AND THE WORKS OF GRACE

Ephesians 2: 4–10 (*continued*)

PAUL closes this passage with a great exposition of that paradox which always lies at the heart of his view of the gospel. That paradox has two arms.

(i) Paul insists that it is by grace that we are saved. We have not earned salvation nor could we have earned it. It is the gift of God and our part is simply to accept it. Paul's point of view is undeniably true; and for two reasons.

(*a*) God is perfection; and, therefore, only perfection is good enough for him. Man by his very nature cannot bring perfection to God; and so, if ever man is to win his way to God, it must always be God who gives and man who takes.

(*b*) God is love; sin is therefore a crime, not against law, but against love. Now it is possible to make atonement for a broken law, but it is impossible to make atonement for a broken heart; and sin is not so much breaking God's law as it is breaking God's heart. Let us take a crude and imperfect analogy. Suppose a motorist by careless driving kills a child. He is arrested, tried, found guilty, sentenced to a term of imprisonment and/or to a fine. After he has paid the fine and served the imprisonment, as far as the law is concerned, the whole matter is over. But it is very different in relation to the mother whose child he killed. He can never put things right with her by serving a term of imprisonment and paying a fine. The only thing which can restore his relationship to her is an act of free forgiveness on her part. That is the way we are to God. It is not God's laws against which we have sinned; it is against his heart. And therefore only an act of free forgiveness of the grace of God can put us back into the right relationship with him.

(ii) That is to say that works have nothing to do with earning salvation. It is neither right nor possible to leave the teaching of Paul here—and yet that is where it is so often left. Paul goes on to say that we are recreated by God for good works. Here is the Pauline paradox. All the good works in the world cannot put us right with God; but there is something radically wrong with the Christianity which does not issue in good works.

There is nothing mysterious about this. It is simply an inevitable law of love. If someone fine loves us, we know that we do not and cannot deserve that love. At the same time we know with utter conviction that we must spend all life in *trying* to be worthy of it.

That is our relationship to God. Good works can never earn salvation; but there is something radically wrong if salvation does not produce good works. It is not that our good works put God in our debt; rather that God's love lays on us the obligation to try throughout all life to be worthy of it.

We know what God wants us to do; God has prepared long beforehand the kind of life He wants us to live, and has told us about it in his book and through his son. We cannot earn God's love; but we can and must show how grateful we are for it, by seeking with our whole hearts to live the kind of life which will bring joy to God's heart.

B.C. AND A.D.

Ephesians 2: 11–22

So then remember, that once, as far as human descent goes, you were Gentiles; you were called the uncircumcision by those who laid claim to that circumcision which is a physical thing, and a thing produced by men's hands. Remember that at that time you had no hope of a Messiah; you were aliens from the society of Israel, and strangers from the covenants on which the promises were based; you had no hope; you were in the world without God. But, as things now are, because of what Christ Jesus has done, you who were once far off have been brought near, at the price of the blood of Christ. For it is he who is our peace; it is he who made both Jew and Gentile into one, and who broke down the middle wall of the barrier between, and destroyed the enmity by coming in the flesh, and wiped out the law of commandments with all its decrees. This he did that in himself he might make the two into one new man, by making peace between them, and that he might reconcile both to God in one body through the Cross, after he had slain the enmity between them by what he did. So he came and preached peace to you who were afar off, and peace to them who were near, because, through him, we both have the right of entry into the presence of the Father, for we come in the one Spirit. So then you are no longer strangers and foreigners resident in a land that is not their own, but you are fellow citizens with God's consecrated people and members of the family of God. It is on the foundation of the prophets and the apostles that you have been built up; and the corner stone is Christ himself. All the building that is going on is being fitted together in him, and it will go on growing until it becomes a holy temple in the Lord, a temple into which you too are built as part, that you may become the dwelling place of God, through the work of the Spirit.

BEFORE CHRIST CAME

Ephesians 2: 11, 12

So then remember, that once, as far as human descent goes, you were Gentiles; you were called the uncircumcision by those who laid claim to that circumcision which is a physical thing, and a thing produced by men's hands. Remember that at that time you had no hope of a Messiah; you were aliens from the society of Israel, and strangers from the covenants on which the promises were based; you had no hope; you were in the world without God.

PAUL speaks of the condition of the Gentiles before Christ came. Paul was the apostle to the Gentiles, but he never forgot the unique place of the Jews in the design and the revelation of God. Here he is drawing the contrast between the life of the Gentile and of the Jew.

(i) The Gentiles were called the uncircumcision by those who laid claim to that circumcision which is a physical and man-made thing. This was the first of the great divisions. The Jew had an immense contempt for the Gentile. They said that the Gentiles were created by God to be fuel for the fires of Hell; that God loved only Israel of all the nations that he had made; that the best of the serpents crushed, the best of the Gentiles killed. It was not even lawful to render help to a Gentile woman in childbirth, for that would be to bring another Gentile into the world. The barrier between Jew and Gentile was absolute. If a Jew married a Gentile, the funeral of that Jew was carried out. Such contact with a Gentile was the equivalent of death; even to go into a Gentile house rendered a Jew unclean. Before Christ the barriers were up; after Christ the barriers were down.

(ii) The Gentiles had no hope of a Messiah. The Authorized Version has it that they were *without Christ*. That is a perfectly possible translation; but the word *Christos* is not primarily a proper name although it has become one. It is an adjective meaning *the anointed one*. Kings on their coronation were anointed; and thus *Christos*, the literal Greek translation of the Hebrew *Messiah*, came to mean the Anointed One of God, the expected King whom God would send into the world to vindicate his own and to bring in the golden age. Even in their bitterest days the Jews never doubted that that Messiah would come. But the Gentiles had no such hope.

See the result of that difference. For the Jew history was

always going somewhere; no matter what the present was like, the future was glorious; the Jewish view of history was essentially optimistic. On the other hand, for the Gentile history was going nowhere. To the Stoics history was cyclic. They believed that it went on for three thousand years; then came a conflagration in which the whole universe was consumed in flames; then the whole process began all over again, and the same events and the same people exactly repeated themselves. To the Gentile history was a progress to nowhere; to the Jew history was a march to God. To the Gentile life was not worth living; to the Jew it was the way to greater life. With the coming of Christ the Gentile entered into that new view of history in which a man is always on the way to God.

HOPELESS AND HELPLESS

Ephesians 2: 11, 12 (*continued*)

(iii) THE Gentiles were aliens from the society of Israel. What does that mean? The name for the people of Israel was *ho hagios láos,* the *holy* people. We have seen that the basic meaning of *hagios* is *different.* In what sense were the people of Israel different from other peoples? In the sense that their only king was God. Other nations might be governed by democracy or aristocracy; Israel was a theocracy. Their governor was God. After his triumphs, the people came to Gideon and offered him the throne of Israel. Gideon's answer was: "I will not rule over you, and my son will not rule over you; the Lord shall rule over you" (*Judges* 8: 23). When the Psalmist sang: "I will extol thee, my God and king" (*Psalm* 145: 1) he meant it literally.

To be an Israelite was to be a member of the society of God; it was to have a citizenship which was divine. Clearly life was going to be completely different for any nation which had a consciousness of destiny like that. It is told that when Pericles, the greatest of the Athenians, was walking forward to

address the Athenian assembly, he used to say to himself:
"Pericles, remember that you are an Athenian and that you
talk to Athenians." For the Jew it was possible to say: "Remember that you are a citizen of God, and that you speak
to the people of God." There is no consciousness of
greatness in all the world like that.

(iv) The Gentiles were strangers from the covenants on
which the promises were based. What does that mean? Israel
was supremely *the covenant people*. What does that mean?
The Jews believed that God had approached their nation with
a special offer. "I will take you for my people, and I will be
your God" (*Exodus* 6: 7). This covenant relationship involved
not only privilege, but also obligation. It involved the keeping
of the law. *Exodus* 24: 1–8 gives us a dramatic picture of
how the Jewish people accepted the covenant and its conditions
—"All the words which the Lord has spoken we will do"
(*Exodus* 24: 3, 7).

If God's design had ever to be worked out, it must be
worked out through a nation. God's choice of Israel was
not favouritism, for it was choice not for special honour but
for special responsibility. But it gave to the Jews the unique
consciousness of being the people of God. Paul could not
forget, because it was a fact of history, that the Jews were
uniquely the instrument in God's hand.

(v) The Gentiles were without hope and without God.
People often speak of the Greeks as being the sunniest people
in history; but there was such a thing as the Greek melan-
choly. At the back of things there was a kind of essential
despair.

Even as far back as Homer that is so. In the *Iliad* (6: 146–149)
Glaucus and Diomede meet in single combat. Before they
close in fight, Diomede wishes to know the lineage of Glaucus,
and Glaucus replies: "Why enquirest thou of my generation?
Even as are the generations of leaves such are those likewise
of men; the leaves that be the wind scattereth upon the
earth, and the forest buddeth and putteth forth more again,
when the season of spring is at hand; so of the generations

of men one putteth forth and another ceaseth." The Greek
could say:

> "We blossom and flourish as leaves on the tree,
> And wither and perish"—

But he could not triumphantly add:

> "But nought changeth Thee."

Theognis could write:

> "I rejoice and disport me in my youth; long enough beneath the
> earth shall I lie, bereft of life, voiceless as a stone, and shall
> leave the sunlight which I loved; good man though I am, then
> shall I see nothing more."

> "Rejoice, O my soul, in thy youth; soon shall other men be in life,
> and I shall be black earth in death."

> "No mortal is happy of all on whom the sun looks down."

In the *Homeric Hymns* the assembly of Olympus is charmed
by the Muses who sing "of the deathless gifts of the gods and
the sorrows of men, even all that they endure by the will of
the immortals, living heedless and helpless, nor can they find
a cure for death, nor a defence against old age."

In Sophocles we find some of the loveliest and the saddest
lines in all history.

> "Youth's beauty fades, and manhood's glory fades.
> Faith dies and unfaith blossoms as a flower;
> Nor ever wilt thou find upon the open streets of men,
> Or secret places of the heart's own love,
> One wind blows true for ever."

It was true that the Gentile was without hope because he
was without God. Israel had always had the radiant hope
in God which burned clearly and inextinguishably even in
her darkest and most terrible days; but in his heart the
Gentile knew only despair, before Christ came to give him hope.

THE END OF BARRIERS
Ephesians 2: 13–18

> But as things now are, because of what Christ Jesus has done,
> you who were once far off have been brought near, at the price

of the blood of Christ. For it is he who is our peace; it is he
who made both Jew and Gentile into one, and who broke down
the middle wall of the barrier between, and destroyed the enmity
by coming in the flesh, and wiped out the law of commandments
with all its decrees. This he did that in himself he might make
the two into one new man, by making peace between them, and
that he might reconcile both to God in one body through the
Cross, after he had slain the enmity by what he did. So he came
and preached peace to you who were afar off, and peace to them
who were near, because, through him, we both have the right of entry
into the presence of the Father, for we come in the one Spirit.

WE have already seen how the Jew hated and despised the
Gentile. Now Paul uses two pictures, which would be specially
vivid to a Jew, to show how that hatred is killed and a
new unity has come.

He says that those who were far off have been brought
near. Isaiah had heard God say: "Peace, peace to the far, and
to the near" (*Isaiah* 57: 19). When the Rabbis spoke about
accepting a convert into Judaism, they said that he had been
brought near. For instance, the Jewish Rabbinic writers tell
how a Gentile woman came to Rabbi Eliezer. She confessed
that she was a sinner and asked to be admitted to the Jewish
faith. "Rabbi," she said, "bring me near." The Rabbi refused.
The door was shut in her face; but now the door was open.
Those who had been far from God were brought near, and
the door was shut to no one.

Paul uses an even more vivid picture. He says that the
middle wall of the barrier between has been torn down.

This is a picture from the Temple. The Temple consisted of
a series of courts, each one a little higher than the one that
went before, with the Temple itself in the inmost of the courts.
First there was the Court of the Gentiles; then the Court of
the Women; then the Court of the Israelites; then the Court
of the Priests; and finally the Holy Place itself.

Only into the first of them could a Gentile come. Between
it and the Court of the Women there was a wall, or rather
a kind of screen of marble, beautifully wrought, and let into it

at intervals were tablets which announced that if a Gentile proceeded any farther he was liable to instant death. Josephus, in his description of the Temple, says: "When you went through these first cloisters unto the second court of the Temple, there was a partition made of stone all round, whose height was three cubits. Its construction was very elegant; upon it stood pillars at equal distances from one another, declaring the law of purity, some in Greek and some in Roman letters that no foreigner should go within the sanctuary" (*The Wars of the Jews*, 5, 5, 2). In another description he says of the second court of the Temple: "This was encompassed by a stone wall for a partition, with an inscription which forbade any foreigner to go in under pain of death" (*The Antiquities of the Jews*, 15, 11, 5). In 1871 one of these prohibiting tablets was actually discovered, and the inscription on it reads: "Let no one of any other nation come within the fence and barrier around the Holy Place. Whosoever will be taken doing so will himself be responsible for the fact that his death will ensue."

Paul well knew that barrier, for his arrest at Jerusalem, which led to his final imprisonment and death, was due to the fact that he had been wrongly accused of bringing Trophimus, an Ephesian Gentile, into the Temple beyond the barrier (*Acts* 21: 28, 29). So then the intervening wall with its barrier shut the Gentile out from the presence of God.

THE EXCLUSIVENESS OF CHRISTLESS HUMAN NATURE

Ephesians 2: 13-18 (*continued*)

IT is not to be thought that the Jews were the only people who put up the barriers and shut people out. The ancient world was full of barriers. There was a time, more than four hundred years before this, when Greece was threatened with invasion by the Persians. It was the golden age of the city state. Greece was made up of famous cities—Athens, Thebes, Corinth and the rest—and it very nearly encountered disaster because the cities refused to co-operate to meet the common threat. "The danger lay," T. R. Glover wrote, "in every generation, in the same fact of single cities, furious for independence at all costs."

Cicero could write much later: "As the Greeks say, all men are divided into two classes—Greeks and barbarians." The Greek called any man a barbarian who could not speak Greek; and they despised him and put up the barriers against him. When Aristotle is discussing bestiality, he says: "It is found most frequently among barbarians," and by barbarians he simply meant non-Greeks. He talks of "the remote tribes of barbarians belonging to the bestial class." The most vital form of Greek religion was the Mystery Religions, and from many of them the barbarian was excluded. Livy writes: "The Greeks wage a truceless war against people of other races, against barbarians." Plato said that the barbarians are "our enemies by nature."

This problem of the barriers is by no means confined to the ancient world. Rita Snowden quotes two very relevant sayings. Father Taylor of Boston used to say: "There is just enough room in the world for all the people in it, but there is no room for the fences which separate them." Sir Philip Gibbs in *The Cross of Peace* wrote: "The problem of fences has grown to be one of the most acute that the world must face. To-day there are all sorts of zig-zag and criss-crossing separating fences running through the races and people of the world. Modern progress has made the world a neighbourhood: God has given us the task of making it a brotherhood. In these days of dividing walls of race and class and creed we must shake the earth anew with the message of the all-inclusive Christ, in whom there is neither bond nor free, Jew nor Greek, Scythian nor barbarian, but all are one."

The ancient world had its barriers. So, too, has our modern world. In any Christless society there can be nothing but middle walls of partition.

THE UNITY IN CHRIST

Ephesians 2: 13–18 (*continued*)

So Paul goes on to say that in Christ these barriers are down. How did Christ destroy them?

(i) Paul says of Jesus, "He is our peace." What did he mean by that? Let us use a human analogy. Suppose two people have a difference and go to law about it; and the experts in the law draw up a document, which states the rights of the case, and ask the two conflicting parties to come together on the basis of that document. All the chances are that the breach will remain unhealed, for peace is seldom made on the basis of a legal document. But suppose that someone whom both of these conflicting parties love comes and talks to them, there is every chance that peace will be made. When two parties are at variance, the surest way to bring them together is through someone whom they both love.

That is what Christ does. *He* is our peace. It is in a common love of him that people come to love each other. That peace is won at the price of his blood, for the great awakener of love is the Cross. The sight of that Cross awakens in the hearts of men of all nations love for Christ, and only when they all love Christ will they love each other. It is not in treaties and leagues to produce peace. There can be peace only in Jesus Christ.

(ii) Paul says of Jesus that he wiped out the law of the commandments with all its decrees. What does that mean? The Jews believed that only by keeping the Jewish law was a man good and able to attain to the friendship and fellowship of God. That law had been worked out into thousands and thousands of commandments and decrees. Hands had to be washed in a certain way; dishes had to be cleaned in a certain way; there was page after page about what could and could not be done on the Sabbath day; this and that and the next sacrifice had to be offered in connection with this and that and the next occasion in life. The only people who fully kept the Jewish law were the Pharisees and there were only six thousand of them. A religion based on all kinds of rules and regulations, about sacred rituals and sacrifices and days, can never be a universal religion. But, as Paul said elsewhere, "Christ is the end of the law" (*Romans* 10: 4). Jesus ended legalism as a principle of religion.

In its place he put love to God and love to men. Jesus came to tell men that they cannot earn God's approbation by a keeping of the ceremonial law but must accept the forgiveness and fellowship which God in mercy freely offers them. A religion based on love can at once be a universal religion.

Rita Snowden tells a story of the war. In France some soldiers with their sergeant brought the body of a dead comrade to a French cemetery to have him buried. The priest told them gently that he was bound to ask if their comrade had been a baptized adherent of the Roman Catholic Church. They said that they did not know. The priest said that he was very sorry but in that case he could not permit burial in his churchyard. So the soldiers took their comrade sadly and buried him just outside the fence. The next day they came back to see that the grave was all right and to their astonishment could not find it. Search as they might they could find no trace of the freshly dug soil. As they were about to leave in bewilderment the priest came up. He told them that his heart had been troubled because of his refusal to allow their dead comrade to be buried in the churchyard; so, early in the morning, he had risen from his bed and with his own hands *had moved the fence* to include the body of the soldier who had died for France.

That is what love can do. The rules and the regulations put up the fence; but love moved it. Jesus removed the fences between man and man because he abolished all religion founded on rules and regulations and brought to men a religion whose foundation is love.

THE GIFTS OF THE UNITY OF CHRIST

Ephesians 2: 13–18 (*continued*)

PAUL goes on to tell of the priceless gifts which come with the new unity in Christ.

(i) He made both Jew and Gentile into one new man.

In Greek there are two words for new. There is *neos* which is new simply in point of time; a thing which is *neos* has come into existence recently, but there may well have been thousands of the same thing in existence before. A pencil produced in the factory this week is *neos*, but there already exist millions exactly like it. There is *kainos* which means new in point of *quality*. A thing which is *kainos* is new in the sense that it brings into the world a new quality of thing which did not exist before.

The word that Paul uses here is *kainos*; he says that Jesus brings together Jew and Gentile and from them both produces one new kind of person. This is very interesting and very significant; it is not that Jesus makes all the Jews into Gentiles, or all the Gentiles into Jews; he produces a new kind of person out of both, although they remain Gentiles and Jews. Chrysostom, famous preacher of the early Church, says that it is as if one should melt down a statue of silver and a statue of lead, and the two should come out gold.

The unity which Jesus achieves is not achieved by blotting out all racial characteristics; it is achieved by making all men of all nations into Christians. It may well be that we have something to learn here. The tendency has always been when we send missionaries abroad to produce people who wear English clothes and speak the English language. There are indeed some missionary churches who would have all their congregations worship with the one liturgy used in the churches at home. It is not Jesus' purpose, however, that we should turn all men into one nation, but that there should be Christian Indians and Christian Africans whose unity lies in their Christianity. The oneness in Christ is in Christ and not in any external change.

(ii) He reconciled both to God. The word Paul uses (*apokatallassein*) is the word used of bringing together friends who have been estranged. The work of Jesus is to show all men that God is their friend and that, therefore, they must be friends with each other. Reconciliation with God involves and necessitates reconciliation with man.

(iii) Through Jesus both Jew and Gentile have the right of access to God. The word Paul uses for *access* is *prosagōgē* and it is a word of many pictures. It is the word used of bringing a sacrifice to God; it is the word used of bringing men into the presence of God that they may be consecrated to his service; it is the word used for introducing a speaker or an ambassador into a national assembly; and above all it is the word used for introducing a person into the presence of a king. There was in fact at the Persian royal court an official called the *prosagōgeus* whose function was to introduce people who desired an audience with the king. It is a priceless boon to have the right to go to some lovely and wise and saintly person at any time; to have the right to break in upon him, to take our troubles, our problems, our loneliness, our sorrow to him. That is exactly the right that Jesus gives us in regard to God.

The unity in Christ produces Christians whose Christianity transcends all their local and racial difference; it produces men who are friends with each other because they are friends with God; it produces men who are one because they meet in the presence of God to whom they all have access.

THE FAMILY AND THE DWELLING-PLACE OF GOD

Ephesians 2: 19–22

So then you are no longer strangers and foreigners resident in a land that is not their own, but you are fellow citizens with God's consecrated people and members of the family of God. It is on the foundation of the prophets and apostles that you have been built up; and the corner stone is Christ himself. All the building that is going on is being fitted together in him, and it will go on growing until it becomes a holy temple in the Lord, a temple into which you too are built as part, that you may become the dwelling-place of God, through the work of the Spirit.

PAUL uses two illuminating pictures. He says that the Gentiles are no longer foreigners but full members of the family of God.

Paul uses the word *xenos* for foreigner. In every Greek city there were *xenoi* and their life was not easy. One wrote home: "It is better for you to be in your own homes, whatever they may be like, than to be in a strange land." The foreigner was always regarded with suspicion and dislike. Paul uses the word *paroikos* for sojourner. The *paroikos* was one step further on. He was a resident alien, a man who had taken up residence in a place but who had never become a naturalized citizen; he paid a tax for the privilege of existing in a land which was not his own. Both the *xenos* and the *paroikos* were always on the fringe.

So Paul says to the Gentiles: "You are no longer among God's people on sufferance. You are full members of the family of God." We may put this very simply; it is through Jesus that we are at home with God.

A. B. Davidson tells how he was in lodgings in a strange city. He was lonely. He used to walk the streets at evening time. Sometimes through an uncurtained window he would see a family sitting round the table or the fire in happy fellowship; then the curtain would be drawn and he would feel shut out, and lonely in the dark.

That is what cannot happen in the family of God. And that is what should never happen in a church. Through Jesus there is a place for all men in the family of God. Men may put up their barriers; churches may keep their Communion tables for their own members. God never does; it is the tragedy of the Church that it is so often more exclusive than God.

The second picture Paul uses is that of a building. He thinks of every church as the part of a great building and of every Christian as a stone built into the Church. Of the whole Church the corner stone is Christ; and the corner stone is what holds everything together.

Paul thinks of this building going on and on, with each part of the building being fitted into Christ. Think of a great cathedral. Down among the foundations there may be a Saxon crypt; on some of the doorways or the windows there may be a Norman arch; one part may be Early English and another Decorated and another Gothic; some may have been added in our own day. There are all kinds of architecture; but the building is a unity because through it all it has been used for the worship of God and for meeting with Jesus Christ.

That is what the Church should be like. Its unity comes not from organization, or ritual, or liturgy; it comes from Christ. *Ubi Christus, ibi ecclesia,* Where Christ is, there is the Church. The Church will realize her unity only when she realizes that she does not exist to propagate the point of view of any body of men, but to provide a home where the Spirit of Christ can dwell and where all men who love Christ can meet in that Spirit.

PRISON AND PRIVILEGES

Ephesians 3: 1–13

To understand the connection of thought in this passage it has to be noted that verses 2–13 are one long parenthesis. The *for this cause* of verse 14 takes up again and resumes the *for this cause* of verse 1. Someone has spoken of Paul's habit of "going off at a word." A single word or idea can send his thoughts off at a tangent. When he speaks of himself as "the prisoner of Christ," it makes him think of the universal love of God and of his part in bringing that love to the Gentiles. In verses 2–13 his thoughts go off on that track; and in verse 14 he comes back to what he meant to say when he began.

It is for this cause that I Paul, the prisoner of Jesus Christ for the sake of you Gentiles—you must have heard of the share that God gave me in dispensing his grace to you, because God's secret was made known to me by direct revelation, as I have just been writing to you, and you can read again what I have just written, if you wish to know what I understand of the meaning of that secret which Christ brought, a secret which was not revealed to the sons of men in other generations as it has now been revealed to his consecrated apostles and prophets by the work of the Spirit. The secret is that the Gentiles are fellow-heirs, fellow-members of the same body, fellow-sharers in the promise in Jesus Christ, through the good news of which I was made a servant through the free gift of the grace of God, which was given to me according to the working of his power. It is to me, who am less than the least of all God's consecrated people, that this privilege has been given—the privilege of preaching to the Gentiles the wealth of Christ, the full story of which no man can ever tell; the privileges of enlightening all men as to what is the meaning of that secret, which was hidden from all eternity, in the God who created all things. It was kept secret up till now in order that now the many-coloured wisdom of God should be made known through the Church to the rulers and powers in the heavenly places; and all this happened and will happen in accordance with the eternal design which he purposed in Jesus Christ, through whom we have a free and confident right of approach to him through faith in him. I therefore pray that you will not lose heart because of my afflictions on your behalf, for these afflictions are your glory.

THE GREAT DISCOVERY

Ephesians 3: 1–7

It is for this cause that I Paul, the prisoner of Jesus Christ for the sake of you Gentiles—you must have heard of the share that God gave me in dispensing his grace to you, because God's secret was made known to me by direct revelation, as I have just been writing to you, and you can read again what I have just written,

if you wish to know what I understand of the meaning of that
secret which Christ brought, a secret which was not revealed to
the sons of men in other generations as it has now been revealed
to his consecrated apostles and prophets by the work of the Spirit.
The secret is that the Gentiles are fellow-heirs, fellow-members of
the same body, fellow-sharers in the promise in Jesus Christ, through
the good news of which I was made a servant through the free
gift of the grace of God, which was given to me according to
the working of his power.

WHEN Paul wrote this letter he was in prison in Rome awaiting
trial before Nero, waiting for the Jewish prosecutors to come
with their bleak faces and their envenomed hatred and their
malicious charges. In prison Paul had certain privileges, for
he was allowed to stay in a house which he himself had
rented and his friends were allowed access to him; but night
and day he was still a prisoner chained to the wrist of the
Roman soldier who was his guard and whose duty it was to
see that Paul would never escape.

In these circumstances Paul calls himself "the prisoner of
Christ." Here is another vivid instance of the fact that the
Christian has always a double life and a double address. Any
ordinary person would have said that Paul was the prisoner
of the Roman government; and so he was. But Paul never
thought of himself as the prisoner of Rome; he always thought
of himself as the prisoner of Christ.

One's point of view makes all the difference in the world.
There is a famous story of the days when Sir Christopher
Wren was building St. Paul's Cathedral. On one occasion
he was making a tour of the work in progress. He came
upon a man at work and asked him: "What are you doing?"
The man said: "I am cutting this stone to a certain size and
shape." He came to a second man and asked him what he was
doing. The man said: "I am earning so much money at my
work." He came to a third man at work and asked him
what he was doing. The man paused for a moment, straightened
himself and answered: "I am helping Sir Christopher Wren
build St. Paul's Cathedral."

If a man is in prison for some great cause he may either grumblingly regard himself as an ill-used creature, or he may radiantly regard himself as the standard-bearer of some great cause. The one regards his prison as a penance; the other regards it as a privilege. When we are undergoing hardship, unpopularity, material loss for the sake of Christian principles we may either regard ourselves as the victims of men or as the champions of Christ. Paul is our example; he regarded himself, not as the prisoner of Nero, but as the prisoner of Christ.

In this section Paul returns to the thought which is at the very heart of this letter. Into his life had come the revelation of the great secret of God. That secret was that the love and mercy and grace of God were meant not for the Jews alone but for all mankind. When Paul had met Christ on the Damascus road there had come to him a sudden flash of revelation. It was to the Gentiles that God had sent him "to open their eyes, that they may turn from darkness to light, and from the power of Satan to God, that they may receive forgiveness of sins, and a place among who are sanctified by faith in me" (*Acts* 26: 18).

This was a completely new discovery. The basic sin of the ancient world was contempt. The Jews despised the Gentiles as worthless in the sight of God. At worst they existed only to be annihilated, "The nation and kingdom that will not serve you shall perish; those nations shall be utterly laid waste" (*Isaiah* 60: 12). At best they existed to be the slaves of Israel; "The wealth of Egypt and the merchandise of Ethiopia and the Sabeans, men of stature, shall come over to you and be yours; they shall come after thee; in chains they shall come over and they shall fall down unto thee" (*Isaiah* 45: 14).

To minds which could think like that it was incredible that the grace and the glory of God were for the Gentiles. The Greek despised the barbarians—and to the Greek all other nations were barbarians. As Celsus said when he was attacking the Christians, "the barbarians may have some gift for discovering truth, but it takes a Greek to understand."

This racial contempt did not end with the ancient world. In the sixteenth century *Complaynt of Scotland*, it is written: "Euere nation reputis vthers nations to be barbarianes, quhen there twa natours and complexions ar contrar till vtheris." In the *Mercantile Marine Magazine* of 1858 there is a recommendation to the effect that the term barbarian should not be applied to British subjects in Chinese official documents. (These two illustrations are taken from *The Stranger at the Gate*, by T. J. Haarhoff.)

But in the ancient world the barriers were complete. No one had ever dreamed that God's privileges were for all people. It was Paul who made that discovery. That is why he is so tremendously important—for, had there been no Paul it is conceivable that there would have been no world-wide Christianity and that we would not be Christians today.

THE SELF-CONSCIOUSNESS OF PAUL

Ephesians 3: 1–7 (*continued*)

WHEN Paul thought of this secret which had been revealed to him, he thought of himself in certain ways.

(i) He regarded himself as the recipient of a new revelation. Paul never thought of himself as having *discovered* the universal love of God; he thought of God having *revealed* it to him. There is a sense in which truth and beauty are always given by God.

It is told that once Sir Arthur Sullivan was at a performance of *H.M.S. Pinafore*. When that lovely duet *"Ah! Leave me not to pine alone"* had been sung, Sullivan turned to the friend sitting beside him and said, "Did I really write that?"

One of the great examples of poetical music of words is Coleridge's *Kubla Khan*. Coleridge fell asleep reading a book in which were the words: "Here Kubla Khan commanded a place to be built and a stately garden thereunto." He dreamed the poem and when he awoke he had nothing to do but write it down.

When a scientist makes a great discovery, over and over again what happens is that he thinks and thinks, and experiments and experiments; and comes to a dead end. Then quite suddenly the solution to his problem flashes upon him. It is given to him—by God.

Paul would never have claimed to be the first man to discover the universality of the love of God; he would have said that God told him the secret which had not been previously revealed to any man.

(ii) He regarded himself as the transmitter of grace. When Paul meets the leaders of the Church to talk over with them his mission to the Gentiles, he talks about the gospel of the uncircumcision being committed to him and of "the grace that was given to me" (*Galatians* 2: 7, 9). When he writes to the Romans, he speaks of "the grace given me by God" (*Romans* 15: 15). Paul saw his task as that of being a channel of God's grace to men. It is one of the great facts of the Christian life that we have been given the precious things of Christianity in order to share them with others. It is one of the great warnings of the Christian life that if we keep them to ourselves we lose them.

(iii) He regarded himself as having the dignity of service. Paul says that he was made a servant by the free gift of the grace of God. He did not think of his service as a wearisome duty but as a radiant privilege. It is often astonishingly difficult to persuade people to serve the Church. To teach for God, to sing for God, to administer affairs for God, to speak for God, to visit those in poverty and distress for God, to give of our time and our talent and our substance for God, should not be counted a duty to be coerced out of us; it is a privilege which we should be glad to accept.

(iv) Paul regarded himself as a sufferer for Christ. He did not expect the way of service to be easy; he did not expect the way of loyalty to be trouble-free. Unamuno, the great Spanish mystic, used to say, "May God deny you peace, and give you glory." F. R. Maltby used to say that Jesus promised his disciples three things—that "they would be

absurdly happy, completely fearless, and in constant trouble."
When the knights of chivalry came to the court of King
Arthur and to the society of the Round Table, they came
asking for dangers to face and dragons to conquer. To suffer
for Christ is not a penalty; it is our glory, for it is to share
in the sufferings of Christ himself and an opportunity to
demonstrate the reality of our loyalty to him.

THE PRIVILEGE WHICH MAKES A MAN HUMBLE

Ephesians 3: 8–13

> It is to me, who am less than the least of all God's consecrated
> people, that this privilege has been given—the privilege of preaching
> to the Gentiles the wealth of Christ, the full story of which no
> man can ever tell; the privilege of enlightening all men as to what
> is the meaning of that secret, which was hidden from all eternity,
> in the God who created all things. It was kept secret up till now
> in order that now the many-coloured wisdom of God should be made
> known through the Church to the rulers and powers in the heavenly
> places; and all this happened and will happen in accordance with
> the eternal design which he purposed in Jesus Christ, through whom
> we have a free and confident approach to him through faith in him.
> I therefore pray that you will not lose heart because of my afflictions
> on your behalf, for these afflictions are your glory.

PAUL saw himself as a man who had been given a double
privilege. He had been given the privilege of discovering the
secret that it was God's will that all men should be gathered
into his love. And he had been given the privilege of making
this secret known to the Church and of being the instrument
by which God's grace went out to the Gentiles. But that
consciousness of privilege did not make Paul proud; it made
him intensely humble. He was amazed that this great privilege
had been given to him who, as he saw it, was less than
the least of God's people.

If ever we are privileged to preach or to teach the message
of the love of God or to do anything for Jesus Christ,

we must always remember that our greatness lies not in ourselves but in our task and in our message. Toscanini was one of the greatest orchestral conductors in the world. Once when he was talking to an orchestra when he was preparing to play one of Beethoven's symphonies with them he said: "Gentlemen, I am nothing; you are nothing; Beethoven is everything." He knew well that his duty was not to draw attention to himself or to his orchestra but to obliterate himself and his orchestra and let Beethoven flow through.

Leslie Weatherhead tells of a talk he had with a public schoolboy who had decided to enter the ministry of the Church. He asked him when he had come to his decision, and the lad said he had been moved to make it after a certain service in the school chapel. Weatherhead very naturally asked who the preacher had been, and the lad answered that he had no idea; he only knew that Jesus Christ had spoken to him that morning. That was true preaching.

The tragic fact is that there are so many who are more concerned with their own prestige than with the prestige of Jesus Christ; and who are more concerned that they should be noticed than that Christ should be seen.

THE PLAN AND THE WISDOM OF GOD

Ephesians 3: 8–13 (*continued*)

THERE are still other things in this passage which we must note.

(i) Paul reminds us that the ingathering of all men was part of the eternal purpose of God. That is something which we would do well to remember. Sometimes the history of Christianity can be presented in such a way that it sounds as if the gospel went out to the Gentiles only because the Jews would not receive it. Paul here reminds us that the salvation of the Gentiles is not an afterthought of God;

the bringing of all men into his love was part of God's eternal design.

(ii) Paul uses a great word to describe the grace of God. He calls it *polupoikilos*, which means *many-coloured*. The idea in this word is that the grace of God will match with any situation which life may bring to us. There is nothing of light or of dark, of sunshine or of shadow, for which it is not triumphantly adequate.

(iii) Again Paul returns to one of his favourite thoughts. In Jesus we have a free approach to God. It sometimes happens that a friend of ours knows some very distinguished person. We ourselves would never have any right to enter into that person's presence; but in our friend's company we have the right of entry. That is what Jesus does for us with God. In his presence there is an open door to God's presence.

(iv) Paul finishes with a prayer that his friends may not be discouraged by his imprisonment. Perhaps they might think that the preaching of the gospel to the Gentiles will be greatly hindered because the champion of the Gentiles is in prison. Paul reminds them that the afflictions through which he is going are for their good.

PAUL'S EARNEST PRAYER

Ephesians 3: 14–21

It is for this cause that I bow my knees in prayer before the Father, of whose fatherhood all heavenly and earthly fatherhood is a copy, that, according to the wealth of his glory, he may grant to you to be strengthened in the inner man, so that Christ through faith may take up his permanent residence in your hearts. I pray that you may have your root and your foundation in love, so that, with all God's consecrated people, you may have the strength fully to grasp the meaning of the breadth and length and depth and height of Christ's love, and to know the love of Christ which is beyond all knowledge, that you may be filled until you reach the fullness of God himself.

To him that is able to do exceeding abundantly, above all that we ask or think, according to the power which works in us, to him be glory in the Church and in Christ Jesus to all generations for ever and ever. Amen.

THE GOD WHO IS FATHER

Ephesians 3: 14–17

It is for this cause that I bow my knees in prayer before the Father, of whose fatherhood all heavenly and earthly fatherhood is a copy, that, according to the wealth of his glory, he may grant to you to be strengthened in the inner man, so that Christ through faith may take up his permanent residence in your hearts.

It is here that Paul begins again the sentence which he began in verse 1 and from which he was deflected. *It is for this cause* begins Paul. What is the cause which makes him pray? We are back again at the basic idea of the letter. Paul has painted his great picture of the Church. This world is a disintegrated chaos; there is division everywhere, between nation and nation, between man and man, within a man's inner life. It is God's design that all the discordant elements should be brought into one in Jesus Christ. But that cannot be done unless the Church carries the message of Christ and of the love of God to every man. It is for that cause that Paul prays. He is praying that the people within the Church may be such that the whole Church will be the body of Christ.

We must note the word used for Paul's attitude in prayer. "I bow my knees," he says, "in prayer to God." That means even more than that he *kneels*; it means that he *prostrates* himself. The ordinary Jewish attitude of prayer was standing, with the hands stretched out and the palms upwards. Paul's prayer for the Church is so intense that he prostrates himself before God in an agony of entreaty.

His prayer is to God the Father. It is interesting to note the different things which Paul says in this letter about God as Father, for from them we get a clearer idea of what was in his mind when he spoke of the fatherhood of God.

(i) God is the Father of Jesus (1: 2, 3; 1: 17; 6: 23). It is not true to say that Jesus was the first person to call God Father. The Greeks called Zeus the father of gods and men; the Romans called their chief god Jupiter, which means *Deus pater*, God the Father. But there are two closely interrelated words which have a certain similarity and yet a wide difference in their meaning.

There is *paternity*. Paternity means fatherhood in the purely physical sense of the term. It can be used of a fatherhood in which the father never even sees the child.

On the other hand there is *fatherhood*. Fatherhood describes the most intimate relationship of love and of fellowship and of care.

When men used the word *father* of God before Jesus came, they used it much more in the sense of paternity. They meant that the gods were responsible for the creation of men. There was in the word none of the love and intimacy which Jesus put into it. The centre of the Christian conception of God is that he is like Jesus, that he is as kind, as loving, as merciful as Jesus was. It was always in terms of Jesus that Paul thought of God.

(ii) God is the Father to whom we have access (2: 18; 3: 12).

The essence of the Old Testament is that God was the person to whom access was forbidden. When Manoah, who was to be the father of Samson, realized who his visitor had been, he said: "We shall surely die, for we have seen God" (*Judges* 13: 22). In the Jewish worship of the Temple the Holy of Holies was held to be the dwelling-place of God and into it only the High Priest might enter, and that only on one day of the year, the Day of Atonement.

The centre of Christian belief is the approachability of God. H. L. Gee tells a story. There was a little boy whose father was promoted to the exalted rank of brigadier. When the little lad heard the news, he was silent for a moment, and then said, "Do you think he will mind if I still call him daddy?" The essence of the Christian faith is unrestricted access to the presence of God.

(iii) God is the Father of glory, the glorious Father (1 : 17). Here is the necessary other side of the matter. If we simply spoke about the accessibility of God, it would be easy to sentimentalize the love of God, and that is exactly what some people do. But the Christian faith rejoices in the wonder of the accessibility of God without ever forgetting his holiness and his glory. God welcomes the sinner, but not if he wishes to trade on God's love in order to remain a sinner. God is holy and those who seek his friendship must be holy too.

(iv) God is the Father of all (4: 6). No man, no Church, no nation has exclusive possession of God; that is the mistake which the Jews made. The fatherhood of God extends to all men, and that means that we must love and respect one another.

(v) God is the Father to whom thanks must be given (5: 20). The fatherhood of God implies the debt of man. It is wrong to think of God as helping us only in the great moments of life. Because God's gifts come to us so regularly we tend to forget that they are gifts. The Christian should never forget that he owes, not only the salvation of his soul, but also life and breath and all things to God.

(vi) God is the pattern of all true fatherhood. That lays a tremendous responsibility on all human fathers. G. K. Chesterton remembered his father only vaguely but his memories were precious. He tells us that in his childhood he possessed a toy theatre in which all the characters were cut-outs in cardboard. One of them was a man with a golden key. He never could remember what the man with the golden key stood for but in his own mind he always connected his father with him, a man with a golden key opening up all kinds of wonderful things.

We teach our children to call God father, and the only

conception of fatherhood they can have is that which we give them. Human fatherhood should be moulded on the fatherhood of God.

THE STRENGTHENING OF CHRIST

Ephesians 3: 14–17 (*continued*)

PAUL prays that his people may be strengthened *in the inner man*. What did he mean? *The inner man* was a phrase by which the Greeks understood three things.

(*a*) There was a man's *reason*. It was Paul's prayer that Jesus Christ should strengthen the reason of his friends. He wanted them to be better able to discern between what was right and what was wrong. He wanted Christ to give them the wisdom which would keep life pure and safe.

(*b*) There was the *conscience*. It was Paul's prayer that the conscience of his people should ever become more sensitive. It is possible to disregard conscience so long that in the end it becomes dulled. Paul prayed that Jesus should keep our consciences tender and on the alert.

(*c*) There was the *will*. So often we know what is right, and mean to do it, but our will is not strong enough to back our knowledge and to carry out our intentions. As John Drinkwater wrote:

> "Grant us the will to fashion as we feel,
>   Grant us the strength to labour as we know,
>   Grant us the purpose, ribbed and edged with steel,
>   To strike the blow.
>
> Knowledge we ask not, knowledge Thou hast lent,
>   But, Lord, the will—there lies our deepest need,
> · Grant us the power to build, above the high intent,
>   The deed, the deed!"

The inner man is the reason, the conscience, the will. The strengthening of the inner man comes when Christ takes up his permanent residence in the man. The word Paul uses for Christ *dwelling* in our hearts is the Greek *katoikein* which is the word used for permanent, as opposed to temporary, residence. Henry Lyte wrote as one of the verses of *Abide with me*:

> "Not a brief glance I beg, a passing word,
> But as Thou dwell'st with Thy disciples, Lord,
> Familiar, condescending, patient, free,
> Come, not to sojourn, but abide with me."

The secret of strength is the presence of Christ within our lives. Christ will gladly come into a man's life—but he will never force his way in. He must await our invitation to bring us his strength.

THE INFINITE LOVE OF CHRIST

Ephesians 3: 18-21

PAUL prays that the Christian may be able to grasp the meaning of the breadth, depth, length and height of the love of Christ. It is as if Paul invited us to look at the universe—to the limitless sky above, to the limitless horizons on every side, to the depth of the earth and of the seas beneath us, and said, "The love of Christ is as vast as that."

It is not likely that Paul had any more definite thought in his mind than the sheer vastness of the love of Christ. But many people have taken this picture and have read meanings, some of them very beautiful, into it. One ancient commentator sees the Cross as the symbol of this love. The upper arm of the Cross points up; the lower arm points down; and the crossing arms point out to the widest horizons. Jerome said that the love of Christ reaches up to include the holy angels; that it reaches down to include even the evil spirits in hell; that in its length it covers the men who are striving on the upward way; and in its breadth it covers the men who are wandering away from Christ.

If we wish to work this out we might say that in the *breadth* of its sweep, the love of Christ includes every man of every kind in every age in every world; in the *length* to which it would go, the love of Christ accepted even the Cross; in its *depth* it descended to experience even death; in its *height*, he still loves us in heaven, where he ever lives to make intercession for us (*Hebrews* 7: 25). No man is outside the love of Christ; no place is outwith its reach.

Then Paul comes back again to the thought which dominates this epistle. Where is that love to be experienced? We experience it *with all God's consecrated people*. That is to say, we find it in the fellowship of the Church. John Wesley's saying was true, "God knows nothing of solitary religion." "No man," he said, "ever went to heaven alone." The Church may have its faults; church members may be very far from what they ought to be; but in the fellowship of the Church we find the love of God.

Paul ends with a doxology and an ascription of praise. God can do for us more than we can dream of, and he does it for us in the Church and in Christ.

Once again, before we leave this chapter, let us think of Paul's glorious picture of the Church. This world is not what it was meant to be; it is torn in sunder by opposing forces and by hatred and strife Nation is against nation, man is against man, class is against class. Within a man's own self the fight rages between the evil and the good. It is God's design that all men and all nations should become one in Christ. To achieve this end Christ needs the Church to go out and tell men of his love and of his mercy. And the Church cannot do that, until its members, joined together in fellowship, experience the limitless love of Christ.

EPHESIANS 4

WITH this chapter the second part of the letter begins. In the first three chapters Paul has dealt with the great and eternal truths of the Christian faith, and with the function of the Church in the plan of God. Now he begins to sketch what each member of the Church must be if the Church is to carry out her part in that plan.

Before we begin this chapter, let us again remind ourselves that the central thought of the letter is that Jesus has brought to a disunited world the way to unity. This way is through faith in him and it is the Church's task to proclaim this message to all the world. And now Paul turns to the character the Christian must have if the Church is to fulfil her great task of being Christ's instrument of universal reconciliation between man and man, and man and God within the world.

WORTHY OF OUR CALLING

Ephesians 4: 1–10

So then, I, the prisoner in the Lord, urge you to behave yourselves in a way that is worthy of the calling with which you are called. I urge you to behave with all humility, and gentleness, and patience. I urge you to bear with one another in love. I urge you eagerly to preserve that unity which the Holy Spirit can bring by binding things together in peace. There is one body and one Spirit, just as you have been called with one hope of your calling. There is one Lord, one faith, one baptism, one God and Father of all, who is above all, and through all, and in all. To each one of you grace has been given, as it has been measured out to you by the free gift of Christ. Therefore scripture says, "He ascended into the height, and brought his captive band of prisoners, and gave gifts to men." (When it says that "he ascended," what else can it mean than that he also descended into the lower parts of the earth? He who descended is the same person as he who ascended above all the heavens, that he might fill all things with his presence.)

THE CHRISTIAN VIRTUES

Ephesians 4: 1–3

So then, I, the prisoner in the Lord, urge you to behave yourselves in a way that is worthy of the calling with which you are called. I urge you to behave with all humility, and gentleness, and patience. I urge you to bear with one another in love. I urge you eagerly to preserve that unity which the Holy Spirit can bring by binding things together in peace.

WHEN a man enters into any society, he takes upon himself the obligation to live a certain kind of life; and if he fails in that obligation, he hinders the aims of his society and brings discredit on its name. Here Paul paints the picture of the kind of life that a man must live when he enters the fellowship of the Christian Church.

The first three verses shine like jewels. Here we have five of the great basic words of the Christian faith.

(i) First, and foremost, there is *humility*. The Greek is *tapeinophrosunē*, and this is actually a word which the Christian faith coined. In Greek there is no word for humility which has not some suggestion of meanness attaching to it. Later Basil was to describe it as "the gem casket of all the virtues"; but before Christianity humility was not counted as a virtue at all. The ancient world looked on humility as a thing to be despised.

The Greek had an adjective for *humble*, which is closely connected with this noun—the adjective *tapeinos*. A word is always known by the company it keeps and this word keeps ignoble company. It is used in company with the Greek adjectives which mean slavish (*andrapodōdēs*, *doulikos*, *douloprepēs*), ignoble (*agennēs*), of no repute (*adoxos*), cringing (*chamaizēlos*, which is the adjective which describes a plant which trails along the ground). In the days before Jesus humility was looked on as a cowering, cringing, servile, ignoble quality; and yet Christianity sets it in the very forefront of the virtues. Whence then comes this Christian humility, and what does it involve?

(*a*) Christian humility comes from *self-knowledge*. Bernard said of it, "It is the virtue by which a man becomes conscious of his own unworthiness, in consequence of the truest knowledge of himself."

To face oneself is the most humiliating thing in the world.

Most of us dramatize ourselves. Somewhere there is a story of a man who before he went to sleep at night dreamed his waking dreams. He would see himself as the hero of some thrilling rescue from the sea or from the flames; he would see himself as an orator holding a vast audience spell-bound; he would see himself walking to the wicket in a Test Match at Lord's and scoring a century; he would see himself in some international football match dazzling the crowd with his skill; always he was the centre of the picture. Most of us are essentially like that. And true humility comes when we face ourselves and see our weakness, our selfishness, our failure in work and in personal relationships and in achievement.

(*b*) Christian humility comes from *setting life beside the life of Christ and in the light of the demands of God.*

God is perfection and to satisfy perfection is impossible. So long as we compare ourselves with second bests, we may come out of the comparison well. It is when we compare ourselves with perfection that we see our failure. A girl may think herself a very fine pianist until she hears one of the world's outstanding performers. A man may think himself a good golfer until he sees one of the world's masters in action. A man may think himself something of a scholar until he picks up one of the books of the great old scholars of encylopaedic knowledge. A man may think himself a fine preacher until he listens to one of the princes of the pulpit.

Self-satisfaction depends on the standard with which we compare ourselves. If we compare ourselves with our neighbour, we may well emerge very satisfactorily from the comparison. But the Christian standard is Jesus Christ and the demands of God's perfection—and against that standard there is no room for pride.

(*c*) There is another way of putting this. R. C. Trench said that humility comes from the constant sense of our own *creatureliness*. We are in absolute dependence on God. As the hymn has it:

> "'Tis Thou preservest me from death
> And dangers every hour;

> I cannot draw another breath
>   Unless Thou give me power.
> My health, my friends, and parents dear
>   To me by God are given;
> I have not any blessing here
>   But what is sent from heaven."

We are creatures, and for the creature there can be nothing but humility in the presence of the creator.

Christian humility is based on the sight of self, the vision of Christ, and the realization of God.

THE CHRISTIAN GENTLEMAN

Ephesians 4: 1–3 (*continued*)

(ii) THE second of the great Christian virtues is what the Authorized Version calls *meekness* and what we have translated *gentleness*. The Greek noun is *praotēs*, the adjective *praus*, and these are beyond translation by any single English word. *Praus* has two main lines of meanings.

(*a*) Aristotle, the great Greek thinker and teacher, has much to say about *praotēs*. It was his custom to define every virtue as the *mean between two extremes*. On one side there was excess of some quality, on the other defect; and in between there was exactly its right proportion. Aristotle defines *praotēs* as the mean between being too angry and never being angry at all. The man who is *praus* is the man who is always angry at the right time and never angry at the wrong time. To put that in another way, the man who is *praus* is the man who is kindled by indignation at the wrongs and the sufferings of others, but is never moved to anger by the wrongs and the insults he himself has to bear. So, then, the man who is (as in the Authorized Version), *meek* is the man who is always angry at the right time but never angry at the wrong time.

(*b*) There is another fact which will illumine the meaning

of this word. *Praus* is the Greek for an animal which has been trained and domesticated until it is completely under control. Therefore the man who is *praus* is the man who has every instinct and every passion under perfect control. It would not be right to say that such a man is entirely self-controlled, for such self-control is beyond human power; but it would be right to say that such a man is God-controlled.

Here then is the second great characteristic of the true member of the Church. He is the man who is so God-controlled that he is always angry at the right time but never angry at the wrong time.

THE UNDEFEATABLE PATIENCE

Ephesians 4: 1-3 (*continued*)

(iii) THE third great quality of the Christian is what the Authorized Version calls *long-suffering*. The Greek is *makrothumia*. This word has two main directions of meaning.

(*a*) It describes the spirit which will never give in and which, because it endures to the end, will reap the reward. Its meaning can best be seen from the fact that a Jewish writer used it to describe what he called "the Roman persistency which would never make peace under defeat." In their great days the Romans were unconquerable; they might lose a battle, they might even lose a campaign, but they could not conceive of losing a war. In the greatest disaster it never occurred to them to admit defeat. Christian patience is the spirit which never admits defeat, which will not be broken by any misfortune or suffering, by any disappointment or discouragement, but which persists to the end.

(*b*) But *makrothumia* has an even more characteristic meaning than that. It is the characteristic Greek word for *patience with men*. Chrysostom defined it as the spirit which has the power to take revenge but never does so. Lightfoot defined it as the spirit which refuses to retaliate. To take a very imperfect analogy—it is often possible to see a puppy and a very large dog together. The puppy yaps at the big dog, worries him, bites him, and all the time the big dog, who could annihilate the puppy with one snap of his teeth, bears the puppy's impertinence with a forbearing dignity. *Makrothumia* is the spirit which bears insult and injury without bitterness and without complaint. It is the spirit which can suffer unpleasant people with graciousness and fools without irritation.

The thing which best of all gives its meaning is that the New Testament repeatedly uses it of God. Paul asks the impenitent sinner if he despises the *patience* of God (*Romans* 2: 4). Paul speaks of the perfect *patience* of Jesus to him (1 *Timothy* 1: 16). Peter speaks of God's *patience* waiting in the days of Noah (1 *Peter* 3: 20). He says that the forbearance of our Lord is our salvation (2 *Peter* 3: 15). If God had been a man, he would long since in sheer irritation have wiped the world out for its disobedience. The Christian must have the patience towards his fellow men which God has shown to him.

THE CHRISTIAN LOVE

Ephesians 4: 1–3 (*continued*)

(iv) THE fourth great Christian quality is *love*. Christian love was something so new that the Christian writers had to invent a new word for it; or, at least, they had to employ a very unusual Greek word—*agapē*.

In Greek there are four words for *love*. There is *erōs*, which is the love between a man and a maid and which involves sexual passion. There is *philia* which is the warm affection which exists between those who are very near and very dear to each other. There is *storgē* which is characteristically the word for family affection. And there is *agapē*, which the Authorized Version translates sometimes *love* and sometimes *charity*.

The real meaning of *agapē* is unconquerable benevolence. If we regard a person with *agapē*, it means that nothing that he can do will make us seek anything but his highest good. Though he injure us and insult us, we will never feel anything but kindness towards him. That quite clearly means that this Christian *love* is not an emotional thing. This *agapē* is a thing, not only of the emotions, but also of the will. It is the ability to retain unconquerable good will to the unlovely and the unlovable, towards those who do not love us, and even towards those whom we do not like. *Agapē* is that quality of mind and heart which compels a Christian never to feel any bitterness, never to feel any desire for revenge, but always to seek the highest good of every man no matter what he may be.

(v) These four great virtues of the Christian life—humility, gentleness, patience, love—issue in a fifth, *peace*. It is Paul's advice and urgent request that the people to whom he is writing should eagerly preserve "the sacred oneness" which should characterize the true Church.

Peace may be defined as *right relationships between man and man*. This oneness, this peace, these right relationships can be preserved only in one way. Every one of the four great Christian virtues depends on the obliteration of self. So long as self is at the centre of things, this oneness can never fully exist. In a society where self predominates, men cannot be other than a disintegrated collection of individualistic and warring units. But when self dies and Christ springs to life within our hearts, then comes the peace, the oneness, which is the great hall-mark of the true Church.

THE BASIS OF UNITY

Ephesians 4: 4–6

There is one body and one Spirit, just as you have been called with one hope of your calling. There is one Lord, one faith, one baptism, one God and Father of all, who is above all, and through all, and in all.

PAUL goes on to set down the basis on which Christian unity is founded.

(i) There is one body. Christ is the head and the Church is the body. No brain can work through a body which is split into fragments. Unless there is a co-ordinated oneness in the body, the designs of the head are frustrated. The oneness of the Church is essential for the work of Christ. That does not need to be a mechanical oneness of administration and of human organization; but it does need to be a oneness founded on a common love of Christ and of every part for the other.

(ii) There is one Spirit. The word *pneuma* in Greek means both *spirit* and *breath*; it is in fact the usual word for breath. Unless the breath be in the body, the body is dead; and the vitalizing breath of the body of the Church is the Spirit of Christ. There can be no Church without the Spirit; and there can be no receiving of the Spirit without prayerful waiting for him.

(iii) There is one hope in our calling. We are all proceeding towards the same goal. This is the great secret of the unity of Christians. Our methods, our organization, even some of our beliefs may be different; but we are all striving towards the one goal of a world redeemed in Christ.

(iv) There is one Lord. The nearest approach to a creed which the early Church possessed was the short sentence: "Jesus Christ is Lord" (*Philippians* 2: 11). As Paul saw it, it was God's dream that there should come a day when all men would make this confession. The word used for Lord is *kurios*. Its two usages in ordinary Greek show us something of what Paul meant. It was used for *master* in contra-distinction to *servant* or *slave*; and it was the regular designation of the Roman Emperor. Christians are joined together because they are all in the possession and in the service of the one Master and King.

(v) There is one faith. Paul did not mean that there is one

creed. Very seldom indeed does the word *faith* mean a *creed* in the New Testament. By faith the New Testament nearly always means the complete commitment of the Christian to Jesus Christ. Paul means that all Christians are bound together because they have made a common act of complete surrender to the love of Jesus Christ. They may describe their act of surrender in different terms; but, however they describe it, that surrender is the one thing common to all of them.

(vi) There is one baptism. In the early Church baptism was usually adult baptism, because men and women were coming direct from heathenism into the the Christian faith. Therefore, before anything else, baptism was a public confession of faith. There was only one way for a Roman soldier to join the army; he had to take the oath that he would be true for ever to his emperor. Similarly, there was only one way to enter the Christian Church—the way of public confession of Jesus Christ.

(vii) There is one God. See what Paul says about the God in whom we believe.

He is the *Father* of all; in that phrase is enshrined the *love* of God. The greatest thing about the Christian God, is not that he is king, not that he is judge, but that he is Father. The Christian idea of God begins in love.

He is *above* all; in that phrase is enshrined the *control* of God. No matter what things may look like God is in control. There may be floods; but "The Lord sits enthroned over the flood" (*Psalm* 29: 10).

He is *through* all; in that phrase is enshrined the *providence* of God. God did not create the world and set it going as a man might wind up a clockwork toy and leave it to run down. God is all through his world, guiding, sustaining, loving.

He is *in* all; in that phrase is enshrined the *presence* of God in all life. It may be that Paul took the germ of this idea from the Stoics. The Stoics believed that God was a fire purer than any earthly fire; and they believed that what gave a man life was that a spark of that fire which was God came and dwelt in his body. It was Paul's belief that in everything there is God.

It is the Christian belief that we live in a God-created, God-controlled, God-sustained, God-filled world.

THE GIFTS OF GRACE

Ephesians 4: 7–10

> To each one of you grace has been given, as it has been measured out to you by the free gift of Christ. Therefore scripture says, "He ascended into the height and brought his captive band of prisoners, and gave gifts to men." (When it says that "he ascended," what else can it mean than that he also descended into the lower parts of the earth? He who descended is the same person as he who ascended above all the heavens, that he might fill all things with his presence.)

PAUL turns to another aspect of his subject. He has been talking about the *qualities* of the members of Christ's Church; now he is going to talk of their *functions* in the Church. He begins by laying down what was for him an essential truth— that every good thing a man has is the gift of the grace of Christ.

> "And every virtue we possess,
>   And every victory won,
>   And every thought of holiness,
>   Are His alone."

To make his point about Christ the giver of gifts, Paul quotes, with a very significant difference, from *Psalm* 68: 18. This Psalm describes a king's conquering return. He ascends on high; that is to say, he climbs the steep road of Mount Zion into the streets of the Holy City. He brings in his captive band of prisoners; that is to say, he marches through the streets with his prisoners in chains behind him to demonstrate his conquering power. Now comes the difference. The Psalm speaks next about the conqueror *receiving* gifts. Paul changes it to read, "*gave* gifts to men."

In the Old Testament the conquering king *demanded and received* gifts from men: in the New Testament the conqueror Christ *offers and gives* gifts to men. That is the essential difference between the two Testaments. In the Old Testament a jealous God insists on tribute from men; in the New Testament a loving God pours out his love to men. That indeed is the good news.

Then, as so often, Paul's mind goes off at a word. He has used the word *ascended,* and that makes him think of Jesus. And it makes him say a very wonderful thing. Jesus *descended* into this world when he entered it as a man; Jesus *ascended* from this world when he left it to return to his glory. Paul's great thought is that the Christ who ascended and the Christ who descended are one and the same person. What does that mean? It means that the Christ of glory is the same as the Jesus who trod this earth; still he loves all men; still he seeks the sinner; still he heals the sufferer; still he comforts the sorrowing; still he is the friend of outcast men and women. As the Scottish paraphrase has it:

> "Though now ascended up on high,
>   He bends on earth a brother's eye;
>   Partaker of the human name,
>   He knows the frailty of our frame.
>
> Our fellow suff'rer yet retains
>   A fellow-feeling of our pains;
>   And still remembers in the skies
>   His tears, His agonies and cries.
>
> In every pang that rends the heart
>   The Man of sorrows has a part;
>   He sympathizes with our grief,
>   And to the suff'rer sends relief."

The ascended Christ is still the lover of the souls of men.

Still another thought strikes Paul. Jesus ascended up on high. But he did not ascend up on high to leave the world; he ascended up on high to fill the world with his presence. When Jesus was here in the flesh, he could only be in one place at one time; he was under all the limitations of the body;

but when he laid this body aside and returned to glory, he was liberated from the limitations of the body and was able then to be everywhere in all the world through his Spirit. To Paul the ascension of Jesus meant not a Christ-deserted but a Christ-filled world.

THE OFFICE-BEARERS OF THE CHURCH

Ephesians 4: 11–13

And he gave to the Church some as apostles, and some as prophets, and some as evangelists, and some as pastors and teachers. This he did that God's consecrated people should be fully equipped, that the work of service might go on, and that the body of Christ should be built up. And this is to go on until we all arrive at complete unity in faith in and knowledge of God, until we reach perfect manhood, until we reach a stature which can be measured by the fullness of Christ.

THERE is a special interest in this passage because it gives us a picture of the organization and the administration of the early Church. In the early Church there were three kinds of office-bearers. There were a few whose writ and authority ran throughout the whole Church. There were many whose ministry was not confined to one place but who carried out a wandering ministry, going wherever the Spirit moved them. There were some whose ministry was a local ministry confined to the one congregation and the one place.

(i) The *apostles* were those whose authority ran throughout the whole Church. The apostles included more than the Twelve. Barnabas was an apostle (*Acts* 14: 4, 14). James, the brother of our Lord, was an apostle (1 *Corinthians* 15: 7; *Galatians* 1: 19). Silvanus was an apostle (1 *Thessalonians* 2: 6). Andronicus and Junias were apostles (*Romans* 16: 7).

For an apostle there were two great qualifications. First, he must have seen Jesus. When Paul is claiming his own rights in face of the opposition of Corinth, he demands: "Am I not an apostle? Have I not seen Jesus our Lord?" (1 *Corinthians* 9: 1). Second, an apostle had to be a witness of the Resurrection and of the Risen Lord. When the eleven met to elect a successor to Judas the traitor, he had to be one who had companied with them throughout the earthly life of Jesus and a witness of the Resurrection (*Acts* 1: 21, 22).

In a sense the apostles were bound to die out, because before so very long those who had actually seen Jesus and who had actually witnessed the Resurrection, would pass from this world. But, in another and still greater sense, the qualification remains. He who would teach Christ must know Christ; and he who would bring the power of Christ to others must have experienced Christ's risen power.

(ii) There were the *prophets*. The prophets did not so much *fore-tell* the future as *forth-tell* the will of God. In forth-telling the will of God, they necessarily to some extent fore-told the future, because they announced the consequences which would follow if men disobeyed that will.

The prophets were wanderers throughout the Church. Their message was held to be not the result of thought and study but the direct result of the Holy Spirit. They had no homes and no families and no means of support. They went from church to church proclaiming the will of God as God had told it to them.

The prophets before long vanished from the Church. There were three reasons why they did so. (*a*) In times of persecution the prophets were the first to suffer; They had no means of concealment and were the first to die for the faith. (*b*) The prophets became a problem. As the Church grew local organization developed. Each congregation began to grow into an organization which had its permanent minister and its local administration. Before long the settled ministry began to resent the intrusion of these wandering prophets, who often disturbed their congregations. The inevitable result was that bit by bit the prophets faded out. (*c*) The office of prophet was singularly liable to abuse. These prophetic wanderers had considerable prestige. Some of them abused their office and made it an excuse for living a very comfortable life at the expense of the congregations whom they visited. The earliest book of church administration is the *Didachē*, *The Teaching of the Twelve Apostles,* which dates back to just after A.D. 100. In it both the prestige and the suspicion of the prophets is clearly seen. The order for the sacrament is given and the prayers to be used are set out; and then comes the instruction that the prophet is to be allowed to celebrate the sacrament as he will. But there are certain other regulations. It is laid down that a wandering prophet may stay one or two days with a congregation, but if he wishes to stay three days he is a false prophet; it is laid down that if any wandering prophet in a moment of alleged inspiration demands money or a meal, he is a false prophet.

(iii) There were the *evangelists.* The evangelists, too, were wanderers. They corresponded to what we would call missionaries. Paul writes to Timothy, "Do the work of an evangelist" (2 *Timothy* 4: 5). They were the bringers of the good news. They had not the prestige and authority of the apostles who had seen the Lord; they had not the influence of the Spirit-inspired prophets; they were the rank and file missionaries of the Church who took the good news to a world which had never heard it.

(iv) There were *the pastors and teachers.* It would seem that this double phrase describes one set of people. In one sense they had the most important task in the whole Church: They were not wanderers but were settled and permanent in the work of one congregation. They had a triple function.

(*a*) They were *teachers.* In the early Church there were few books. Printing was not to be invented for almost another fourteen hundred years. Every book had to be written by hand and a book the size of the New Testament would cost as much as a whole year's wages for a working man. That meant that the story of Jesus had mainly to be transmitted by word of mouth. The story of Jesus was told long before it was written down; and these teachers had the tremendous responsibility of being the respositories of the gospel story. It was their function to know and to pass on the story of the life of Jesus.

(b) The people who came into the Church were coming straight from heathenism; they knew literally nothing about Christianity, except that Jesus Christ had laid hold upon their hearts. Therefore these teachers had to open out the Christian faith to them. They had to explain the great doctrines of the Christian faith. It is to them that we owe it that the Christian faith remained pure and was not distorted as it was handed down.

(c) These teachers were also *pastors*. *Pastor* is the Latin word for a *shepherd*. At this time the Christian Church was no more than a little island in a sea of paganism. The people who came into it were only one remove from their heathen lives; they were in constant danger of relapsing into heathenism; and the duty of the pastor was to shepherd his flock and keep them safe.

The word is an ancient and an honourable one. As far back as Homeric times Agamemnon the king was called the Shepherd of the People. Jesus had called himself the Good Shepherd (*John* 10: 11, 14). The writer to the Hebrews called Jesus the great shepherd of the sheep (*Hebrews* 13: 20). Peter called Jesus the shepherd of men's souls (1 *Peter* 2: 25). He called him the Chief Shepherd (1 *Peter* 5: 4). Jesus had commanded Peter to tend his sheep (*John* 21: 16). Paul had warned the elders of Ephesus that they must guard the flock whom God had committed to their care (*Acts* 20: 28). Peter had exhorted the elders to tend the flock of God (1 *Peter* 5: 2).

The picture of the shepherd is indelibly written on the New Testament. He was the man who cared for the flock and led the sheep into safe places; he was the man who sought the sheep when they wandered away and, if need be, died to save them. The shepherd of the flock of God is the man who bears God's people on his heart, who feeds them with the truth, who seeks them when they stray away, and who defends them from all that would hurt their faith. And the duty is laid on every Christian that he should be a shepherd to all his brethren.

THE AIM OF THE OFFICE-BEARER

Ephesians 4: 11–13 *(continued)*

AFTER Paul has named the different kinds of office-bearers within the Church, he goes on to speak of their aim and of what they must try to do.

Their aim is that the members of the Church should be fully equipped. The word Paul uses for *equipped* is interesting. It is *katartismon,* which comes from the verb *katartizein.* The word is used in surgery for setting a broken limb or for putting a joint back into its place. In politics it is used for bringing together opposing factions so that government can go on. In the New Testament it is used of mending nets (*Mark* 1: 19), and of disciplining an offender until he is fit to take his place again within the fellowship of the Church (*Galatians* 6: 1). The basic idea of the word is that of putting a thing into the condition in which it ought to be. It is the function of the office-bearers of the Church to see that the members of the Church are so educated, so guided, so cared for, so sought out when they go astray, that they become what they ought to be.

Their aim is that the work of service may go on. The word used for service is *diakonia;* and the main idea which lies behind this word is that of *practical service.* The office-bearer is not to be a man who simply talks on matters of theology and of Church law; he is in office to see that practical service of God's poor and lonely people goes on.

Their aim is to see to it that the body of Christ is built up. Always the work of the office-bearer is construction, not destruction. His aim is never to make trouble, but always to see that trouble does not rear its head; always to strengthen, and never to loosen, the fabric of the Church.

The office-bearer has even greater aims. These may be said to be his immediate aims; but beyond them he has still greater aims.

His aim is that the members of the Church should arrive at perfect unity. He must never allow parties to form in the

Church nor do anything which would cause differences in it. By precept and example he must seek to draw the members of the Church into a closer unity every day.

His aim is that the members of the Church should reach perfect manhood. The Church can never be content that her members should live decent, respectable lives; her aim must be that they should be examples of perfect Christian manhood and womanhood.

So Paul ends with an aim without peer. The aim of the Church is that her members should reach a stature which can be measured by the fullness of Christ. The aim of the Church is nothing less than to produce men and women who have in them the reflection of Jesus Christ himself. During the Crimean War Florence Nightingale was passing one night down a hospital ward. She paused to bend over the bed of a sorely wounded soldier. As she looked down, the wounded lad looked up and said: "You're Christ to me." A saint has been defined as "someone in whom Christ lives again." That is what the true Church member ought to be.

GROWING INTO CHRIST

Ephesians 4: 14–16

> All this must be done so that we should no longer be infants in the faith, wave-tossed and blown hither and thither by every wind of teaching, by the clever trickery of men, by cunning cleverness designed to make us take a wandering way. Instead of that it is all designed to make us cherish the truth in love, and to make us grow in all things into him who is the head—it is Christ I mean. It is from Christ that the whole body is fitted and united together, by means of all the joints which supply its needs, according as each part performs the share of the task allotted to it. It is from him that the body grows and builds itself up in love.

IN every Church there are certain members who must be protected. There are those who are like children, they are dominated by a desire for novelty and the mercy of the latest fashion in religion. It is the lesson of history that popular fashions in religion come and go but the Church continues for ever. The solid food of religion is always to be found within the Church.

In every Church there are certain people who have to be guarded against. Paul speaks of the clever trickery of men; the word he uses *(kubeia)* means skill in manipulating the dice. There are always those who by ingenious arguments seek to lure people away from their faith. It is one of the characteristics of our age that people talk about religion more than they have done for many years; and the Christian, especially the young Christian, has often to meet the clever arguments of those who are against the Church and against God.

There is only one way to avoid being blown about by the latest religious fashion and to avoid being seduced by the specious arguments of clever men, and that is by continual growth into Christ.

Paul uses still another picture. He says that a body is only healthy and efficient when every part is thoroughly co-ordinated. Paul says that the Church is like that; and the Church can be like that only when Christ is really the head and when every member is moving under his control, just as every part of a healthy body is obedient to the brain.

The only thing which can keep the individual Christian solid in the faith and secure against seduction, the only thing which can keep the Church healthy and efficient, is an intimate connection with Jesus Christ who is the head and the directing mind of the body.

THE THINGS WHICH MUST BE ABANDONED

Ephesians 4: 17–24

I say this and I solemnly lay it upon you in the Lord—you must no longer live the kind of life the Gentiles live, for their minds are concerned with empty things; their understandings are darkened; they are strangers from the life God gives, because of the ignorance that is in them and because of the petrifying of their hearts. They have come to a stage when they are past feeling; and in their shameless wantonness they have abandoned themselves to every kind of unclean conduct in the insatiable lust of their desires. But that is not the way that you have learned Christ, if indeed you have really listened to him, and have been taught in him, as the true teaching in Jesus is. You must stop living in your former way of life. You must put off your old manhood, which is perishing, as deceitful desires are bound to make it do. You must be renewed in the spirit of your minds. You must put on the new manhood, created after God's pattern, in righteousness and in true holiness.

PAUL appeals to his converts to leave their old way of life and to turn to Christ's. In this passage he picks out what he considers the essential characteristics of heathen life. The heathen are concerned with empty things which do not matter; their minds are darkened because of their ignorance. Then comes the salient word; their hearts are *petrified*.

The word which Paul uses for the *petrifying* of their hearts is grim and terrible. It is *pōrōsis*. *Pōrōsis* comes from *pōros*, which originally meant a stone that was harder than marble. It came to have certain medical uses. It was used for the chalk stone which can form in the joints and completely paralyse action. It was used of the callus that forms where a bone has been broken and re-set, a callus which is harder than the bone itself. Finally the word came to mean the loss of all power of sensation; it described something which had become so hardened, so petrified that it had no power to feel at all.

That is what Paul says the heathen life is like. It has become so hardened that it has lost the power of feeling. In the *Epistle to a Young Friend*, Robert Burns wrote about sin:

> "I waive the quantum o' the sin,
>   The hazard of concealing;
>   But och! it hardens a' within,
>   And petrifies the feeling!"

The terror of sin is its petrifying effect. The process of sin is quite discernible. No man becomes a great sinner all at once.

At first he regards sin with horror. When he sins, there enters into his heart remorse and regret. But if he continues to sin there comes a time when he loses all sensation and can do the most shameful things without any feeling at all. His conscience is petrified.

Paul uses two other terrible Greek words to describe the heathen way of life. He says that they have abandoned themselves to every kind of unclean conduct in *the insatiable lust of their desires;* and that they have done so in their *shameless wantonness.*

The word for shameless wantonness is *aselgeia.* It is defined by Plato as "impudence"; and by another writer as "preparedness for every pleasure." It is defined by Basil as "a disposition of the soul incapable of bearing the pain of discipline." The great characteristic of *aselgeia* is this—the bad man usually tries to hide his sin; but the man who has *aselgeia* in his soul does not care how much he shocks public opinion so long as he can gratify his desires. Sin can get such a grip of a man that he is lost to decency and shame. He is like a drug taker who first takes the drug in secret, but comes to a stage when he openly pleads for the drug on which he has become dependent. A man can become such a slave of liquor that he does not care who sees him drunk. A man can let his sexual desires so master him that he does not care who sees him satisfy them.

The Christless man does all this in the *insatiable lust of his desires.* The word is *pleonexia,* another terrible word, which the Greeks defined as "arrogant greediness," as "the accursed love of possessing," as "the unlawful desire for the things which belong to others." It has been defined as the spirit in which a man is always ready to sacrifice his neighbour to his own desires. *Pleonexia* is the irresistible desire to have what we have no right to possess. It might issue in the theft of material things; it might issue in the spirit which tramples on other people to get its own way; it might issue in sexual sin.

In the heathen world, Paul saw three terrible things. He saw men's hearts so petrified that they were not even aware that they were sinning; he saw men so dominated by sin that shame was lost and decency forgotten; he saw men so much at the mercy of their desires that they did not care whose life they injured and whose innocence they destroyed so long as these desires were satisfied. These are exactly the sins of the Christless world today, sins that can be seen invading life at every point and stalking the streets of every great city.

Paul urges his converts to have done with that kind of life. He uses a vivid way of speaking. He says: "Put off your old way of life as you would put off an old suit of clothes; clothe yourself in a new way; put off your sins, and put on the righteousness and the holiness which God can give you."

THINGS WHICH MUST BE BANISHED FROM LIFE

Ephesians 4: 25–32

> So then strip yourselves of falsehood, and let each of you speak the truth with his neighbour, because we are all members of the same body. Be angry—but be angry in such a way that your anger is not a sin. Do not let the sun set on your wrath, and do not give the devil any opportunity. Let him who was a thief steal no more; rather let him take to hard work, and to producing good with his hands, in order that he may be able to share with the man who is in need. Do not allow any foul word to issue from your mouth; but let your words be good, designed for necessary edification, that they may bring benefit to those who hear them. Do not grieve the Holy Spirit of God, with whom you are sealed until the day of your redemption comes. Let all bitterness, all outbreaks of passion, all long-lived anger, all loud talking, all insulting language be removed from you with all evil. Show yourselves kind to one another, merciful, forgiving one another, as God in Christ forgave you.

PAUL has just been saying that when a man becomes a Christian, he must put off his old life as a man puts off a coat for which he has no further use. Here he speaks of the things which must be banished from the Christian life.

(i) There must be no more falsehood. There is more than one kind of lie in this world.

There is the lie of speech, sometimes deliberate and sometimes almost unconscious. Dr. Johnson has an interesting bit of advice in regard to the bringing up of children. "Accustom your children constantly to this (the telling of the truth); if a thing happened at one window, and they, when relating it, say that it happened at another, do not let it pass, but instantly check them; you do not know where deviation from truth will end. . . . It is more from carelessness about truth than from intentional lying, that there is so much falsehood in the world." Truth demands a deliberate effort.

There is also the lie of silence, and maybe it is even commoner. André Maurois, in a memorable phrase, speaks of "the menace of things unsaid." It may be that in some discussion a man by his silence gives approval to some course of action which he knows is wrong. It may be that a man withholds warning or rebuke when he knows quite well he should have given it.

Paul gives the reason for telling the truth. It is because we are all members of the same body. We can live in safety only because the senses and the nerves pass true messages to the brain. If they took to passing false messages, if, for instance, they told the brain that something was cool and touchable when in fact it was hot and burning, life would very soon come to an end. A body can function healthily only when each part of it passes true messages to the brain. If then we are all bound into one body, that body can function properly only when we speak the truth.

(ii) There must be anger in the Christian life, but it must be the right kind of anger. Bad temper and irritability are without defence; but there is an anger without which the world would be a poorer place. The world would have lost much without the blazing anger of Wilberforce against the slave trade or of Shaftesbury against the labour conditions of the nineteenth century.

There was a certain rugged bluntness about Dr. Johnson.

When he thought a thing was wrong, he said so with force. When he was about to publish the *Tour to the Hebrides*, Hannah More asked him to mitigate some of its asperities. She tells that his answer was that "he would not cut off his claws, nor make his tiger a cat, to please anybody." There is a place for the tiger in life; and when the tiger becomes a tabby cat, something is lost.

There were times when Jesus was terribly and majestically angry. He was angry when the scribes and Pharisees were watching to see if he would heal the man with the withered hand on the Sabbath day (*Mark* 3: 5). It was not their criticism of himself at which he was angry; he was angry that their rigid orthodoxy desired to impose unnecessary suffering on a fellow creature. He was angry when he made a whip and drove the changers of money and the sellers of victims from the Temple courts (*John* 2: 13–17).

F. W. Robertson of Brighton tells in one of his letters that he bit his lips until they bled when he met on the street a certain man whom he knew to be luring a pure young girl to destruction. John Wesley said: "Give me a hundred men who fear nothing but God, and *who hate nothing but sin,* and who know nothing but Jesus Christ and him crucified, and I will shake the world."

The anger which is selfish and uncontrolled is a sinful and hurtful thing, which must be banished from the Christian life. But the selfless anger which is disciplined into the service of Christ and of our fellow men is one of the great dynamic forces of the world.

THINGS WHICH MUST BE BANISHED FROM LIFE

Ephesians 4: 25–32 *(continued)*

(iii) PAUL goes on to say that the Christian must never let the sun set upon his wrath. Plutarch tells us that the disciples of Pythagoras had a rule of their society, that if, during the day, anger had made them speak insultingly to each other, before the sun set they shook hands and kissed each other and were reconciled. There was a Jewish Rabbi whose prayer it was that he might never go to sleep with any bitter thought against a brother man within his mind.

Paul's advice is sound, because the longer we postpone mending a quarrel, the less likely we are ever to mend it. If there is trouble between us and anyone else, if there is trouble in a Church or a fellowship or any society where men meet, the only way to deal with it is at once. The longer it is left to flourish, the more bitter it will grow. If we have been in the wrong, we must pray to God to give us grace to admit that it was so; and even if we have been right, we must pray to God to give us the graciousness which will enable us to take the first step to put matters right.

Along with this phrase Paul puts another command. The Greek can equally well mean two things. It can mean: "Don't give the devil his opportunity." An unhealed breach is a magnificent opportunity for the devil to sow dissension. Many a time a Church has been torn into factions because two people quarrelled and let the sun set upon their wrath. But there is another meaning which this phrase can have. The word for devil in Greek is *diabolos;* but *diabolos* is also the normal Greek for a *slanderer.* Luther, for instance, took this to mean: "Give the slanderer no place in your life." It may well be that this is the true meaning of what Paul wishes to say. No one in this world can do more damage than the slanderous tale-bearer. As Coleridge wrote in *Christabel:*

> "Alas! they had been friends in youth;
>   But whispering tongues can poison truth,"

There are reputations murdered over the teacups every day; and when a man sees a tale-bearer coming, he would do well to shut the door in his face.

(iv) The man who was a thief must become an honest workman. This was necessary advice, for in the ancient world thieving was rampant. It was very common in two places, at the docks and above all in the public baths. The public baths were the clubs of the time; and stealing the belongings of the bathers was one of the commonest crimes in any Greek city.

The interesting thing about this saying is the reason Paul gives for being an honest workman. He does not say: "Become an honest workman so that you may support yourself." He says: "Become an honest workman so that you may have something to give away to those who are poorer than yourself." Here is a new idea and a new ideal—that of working in order to give away.

James Agate, tells of a letter from Arnold Bennett, the famous novelist, to a less fortunate writer. Bennett was an ambitious and in many ways a worldly man; but in this letter to a fellow writer whom he hardly knew, he says: "I have just been looking at my bankbook; and I find that I have a hundred pounds which I don't need; I am sending you a cheque herewith for that amount."

In modern society no man has overmuch to give away but we do well to remember the Christian ideal is that we work, not to amass things, but to be able, if need be, to give them away.

(v) Paul forbids all foul-mouthed speaking; and then goes on to put the same thing positively. The Christian should be characterized by words which help his fellow men. As Moffatt translates it, Eliphaz the Temanite paid Job a tremendous compliment. "Your words," he said, "have kept men on their feet" (*Job* 4: 4). Such are the words that every Christian ought to speak.

(vi) Paul urges us not to grieve the Holy Spirit. The Holy Spirit is the guide of life. When we act contrary to the counsel of our parents when we are young, we hurt them. Similarly, to act contrary to the guidance of the Holy Spirit is to grieve the Spirit and to hurt the heart of God, the Father, who, through the Spirit, sent his word to us.

THINGS WHICH MUST BE BANISHED FROM LIFE

Ephesians 4: 25–32 *(continued)*

PAUL ends this chapter with a list of things which must go from life.

(*a*) There is *bitterness (pikria)*. The Greeks defined this word as *long-standing resentment,* as the spirit which refuses to be reconciled. So many of us have a way of nursing our wrath to keep it warm, of brooding over the insults and the injuries which we have received. Every Christian might well pray that God would teach him how to forget.

(*b*) There are *outbreaks of passion (thumos)* and *long-lived anger (orgē)*. The Greeks defined *thumos* as the kind of anger which is like the flame which comes from straw; it quickly blazes up and just as quickly subsides. On the other hand, they described *orgē* as anger which has become habitual. To the Christian the burst of temper and the long-lived anger are both alike forbidden.

(*c*) There is *loud talking* and *insulting language*. A certain famous preacher tells how his wife used to advise him, "In the pulpit, keep your voice down." Whenever, in any discussion or argument, we become aware that our voice is raised, it is time to stop. The Jews spoke about what they called "the sin of insult," and maintained that God does not hold him guiltless who speaks insultingly to his brother man.

Lear said of Cordelia:

> "Her voice was ever soft,
> Gentle and low, an excellent thing in woman."

It would save a great deal of heartbreak in this world if we simply learned to keep our voices down and if, when we had nothing good to say to a person, we did not say anything at all. The argument which has to be supported in a shout is no argument; and the dispute which has to be conducted in insults is not an argument but a brawl.

So Paul comes to the summing up of his advice. He tells us to be *kind (chrēstos)*. The Greeks defined this quality as the disposition of mind which thinks as much of its neighbour's affairs as it does of its own. Kindness has learned the secret of looking outwards all the time, and not inwards. He tells us to forgive others as God forgave us. So, in one sentence, Paul lays down the law of personal relationships—that we should treat others as Jesus Christ has treated us.

THE IMITATION OF GOD

Ephesians 5: 1–8

You must become imitators of God, as well loved children imitate their father. You must live in love, as Christ loved you, and gave himself to God as a sacrifice and an offering, a sacrifice which was the odour of a sweet savour to God. Let no one even mention fornication and unclean living and insatiable desire among you—it does not befit God's consecrated people to talk about things like that. Let no one even mention shameful conduct. Let there be no foolish talking and graceless jesting among you—for these things are not fitting for people like you. But rather let your talk be a gracious thanksgiving to God. You know this and you are well aware of it, that no fornicator, no unclean liver, no one who gives rein to insatiate desire—which is idolatry—has any share in the kingdom of Christ and God. Let no one deceive you with empty words. It is because of these vices that the wrath of God comes upon the children of disobedience. Don't become partners with them.

PAUL sets before his Christian people the highest standard in all the world; he tells them they must be imitators of God. Later Clement of Alexandria was to say daringly that the true Christian wise man practises being God. When Paul talked of imitation he was using language which the wise men of Greece could understand. *Mimēsis, imitation,* was a main part in the training of an orator. The teachers of rhetoric declared that the learning of oratory depended on three things—theory, imitation and practice. The main part of their training was the study and the imitation of the masters who had gone before. It is as if Paul said: "If you were to train to be an orator, you would be told to imitate the masters of speech. Since you are training in life, you must imitate the Lord of all good life."

Above all the Christian must imitate the love and the forgiveness of God. Paul uses a typical Old Testament phrase, "odour of a sweet savour," which goes back to a very old idea, as old as sacrifice itself. When a sacrifice was offered on an altar, the odour of the burning meat went up to heaven and the god to whom the sacrifice was offered was supposed to feast upon that odour. A sacrifice which had the odour of a sweet savour was specially pleasing and specially acceptable to the god to whom it was offered.

Paul takes the old phrase which time had hallowed—it occurs almost fifty times in the Old Testament—and uses it of the sacrifice that Jesus brought to God. The sacrifice of Jesus was well-pleasing to God.

What was that sacrifice? It was a life of perfect obedience to God and of perfect love to men, an obedience so absolute and a love so infinite that they accepted the Cross. What Paul says is: "Imitate God. And you can do so only by loving men with the same sacrificial love with which Jesus loved them and forgiving them in love as God has done."

Paul goes on to another matter. It has been said that chastity was the one new virtue which Christianity introduced into the world. It is certainly true that the ancient world regarded sexual immorality so lightly that it was no sin at all. It was the expected thing that a man should have a mistress. In places like Corinth the great temples were staffed by hundreds of priestesses who were sacred prostitutes and whose earnings went to the upkeep of the Temple.

In his speech *Pro Caelio* Cicero pleads: "If there is anyone who thinks that young men should be absolutely forbidden the love of courtesans, he is indeed extremely severe. I am not able to deny the principle that he states. But he is at variance not only with the licence of what our own age allows but also with the customs and concessions of our ancestors. When indeed was this not done? When did anyone ever find fault with it? When was such permission denied? When was it that that which is now lawful was not lawful?"

The Greeks said that Solon was the first person to allow the introduction of prostitutes into Athens and then the building of brothels; and with the profits of the new trade a new Temple was built to Aphrodite, the goddess of love. Nothing could show the Greek point of view better than the fact that they saw nothing wrong in building a temple to the gods with the proceeds of prostitution.

When Paul set this stress on moral purity, he was erecting a standard which the ordinary heathen had never dreamed of. That is why he pleads with them so earnestly and lays down his laws of purity with such stringency. We must remember the kind of society from which these Christian converts had come and the kind of society with which they were encompassed. There is nothing in all history like the moral miracle which Christianity wrought.

JESTING ABOUT SIN

Ephesians 5: 1–8 *(continued)*

WE must note two other warnings which Paul gives.

(i) He says that these shameful sins are not even to be talked about. The Persians had a rule, so Herodotus tells us, by which "it was not even allowed to speak such things as it was not allowed to do." To jest about a thing or to make it a frequent subject of conversation is to introduce it into the mind and to bring nearer the actual doing of it. Paul warns that some things are not safe even to talk or to jest about. It is a grim commentary on human nature that many a book and many a play and many a film has had success simply because it dealt with forbidden and ugly things.

(ii) He says that his converts must not allow themselves to be deceived with empty words. What does he mean? There were voices in the ancient world, even in the Christian Church, which taught men to think lightly of bodily sin.

In the ancient world there was a line of thought called Gnosticism. Gnosticism began from the contention that spirit alone is good and that matter is always evil. If that be so, it follows that only spirit is to be valued and that matter must be utterly despised. Now a man is composed of two parts; he is *body* and *spirit*. According to this point of view only his spirit matters; his body is of no importance whatsoever. Therefore, some at least of the Gnostics went on to argue, it does not matter what a man does with his body. It will make no difference if he gluts its desires. Bodily and sexual sin were of no importance because they were of the body and not of the spirit.

Christianity met such teaching with the contention that body and soul are equally important. God is the creator of both, Jesus Christ for ever sanctified human flesh by taking it upon himself, the body is the temple of the Holy Spirit and Christianity is concerned with the salvation of the whole man, body, soul and spirit.

(iii) That attack came from outside the Church; but an even more dangerous attack came from inside. There were those in the Church who perverted the doctrine of grace.

We hear the undertones of Paul's argument with them in *Romans* 6. Their argument ran like this. "Do you say that God's grace is the greatest thing in all the world?" "Yes." "Do you say that God's grace is wide enough to cover every sin?" "Yes." "Then let us go on sinning, for God's grace can wipe out every sin. In fact the more we sin the more chances God's grace will get to operate."

Christianity met that argument by insisting that grace was not only a privilege and a gift; it was a responsibility and an obligation. It was true that God's love could and would forgive; but the very fact that God loves us lays on us the obligation to deserve that love as best we can.

The gravest disservice any man can do to a fellow man is to make him think lightly of sin. Paul pleaded with his converts not to be deceived with empty words which took the horror from the idea of sin.

THE CHILDREN OF LIGHT

Ephesians 5: 9–14

> For once you were darkness, but now you are light in the Lord. You must behave as children of the light, for the fruit of light consists in all benevolence and righteousness and truth. You must decide what is well-pleasing to the Lord. You must take no share in the barren works of the dark. Rather you must expose them, for it is a shameful thing even to speak about the hidden things which are done in secret by such men. Whatever is exposed to the light is illuminated. And everything which is illuminated becomes light. That is why it says: "Wake, O sleeper, and rise from the dead, and Christ will shine upon you."

PAUL saw the heathen life as life in the dark; and the Christian life as life in the light. So vividly does he wish to put this that he does not say the heathen are children of the dark and the Christians children of the light; he says the heathen *are* dark and the Christians *are* light. He has certain things to say about the light which Jesus Christ brings to men.

(i) The light produces good fruit. It produces benevolence, righteousness and truth. Benevolence *(agathōsunē)* is a certain generosity of spirit. The Greeks themselves defined righteousness *(dikaiosunē)* as "giving to men and to God that which is their due." Truth *(alētheia)* is not in New Testament thought simply an intellectual thing to be grasped with the mind; it is moral truth, not only something to be *known* but something to be *done*. The light which Christ brings makes us useful citizens of this world; it makes us men and women who never fail in duty, human or divine; it makes us strong to do that which we know is true.

(ii) The light enables us to discriminate between that which is well-pleasing and that which is not pleasing to God. It is in the light of Christ that all motives and all actions must be tested. In the bazaars of the east the shops are often simply little covered enclosures with no windows. A man might wish to buy a piece of silk or an article of beaten brass. Before he buys it he takes it out to the street and holds it up to the sun, so that the light might reveal any flaws which happen to be in it. It is the Christian's duty to expose every action, every decision, every motive to the light of Christ.

(iii) The light exposes that which is evil. The best way to rid the world of any evil is to drag it into the light. So long as the thing is being done in secret, it goes on; but when it is taken into the light of day, it dies a natural death. The surest way to cleanse the depths of our own hearts and the practices of any society in which we happen to be involved is to expose them to the light of Christ.

(iv) Finally, Paul says: "Everything which is illuminated becomes light." What he seems to mean is that light has in itself a cleansing quality. In our own generation we know that many a disease has been conquered simply by letting the sunlight in. The light of Christ is like that. We must never think of the light of Christ as only condemnatory; it is a healing thing too.

Paul finishes this passage with a quotation in poetry. In Moffatt's translation it runs:

> "Wake up, O sleeper, and rise from the dead;
> So Christ will shine upon you."

Paul introduces the quotation as if everybody knew it, but no one now knows where it came from. There are certain interesting suggestions.

Almost certainly, being in poetry, it is a fragment of an early Christian hymn. It may well have been part of a baptismal hymn. In the early Church nearly all baptisms were of adults, confessing their faith as they came out of heathenism into Christianity. Perhaps these were the lines which were sung as they arose from the water, to symbolize the passage from the dark sleep of paganism to the awakened life of the Christian way.

Again, it has been suggested that these lines are part of a hymn, which was supposed to give the summons of the archangel when the last trumpet sounded over the earth. Then would be the great awakening when men rose from the sleep of death to receive the eternal life of Christ.

These things are speculations, but it seems certain that when we read these lines, we are reading a fragment of one of the first hymns the Christian Church ever sang.

THE CHRISTIAN FELLOWSHIP

Ephesians 5: 15–21

Be very careful how you live. Do not live like unwise men, but like wise men. Use your time with all economy for these are evil days. That is the reason why you must not be senseless, but you must understand what the will of God is. Do not get drunk with wine—that is profligacy—but be filled with the Spirit. Speak to each other in psalms and hymns and songs the Spirit teaches you. Let the words and the music of your praise to God come from your heart. Give thanks for all things at all times to God the Father in the name of our Lord Jesus Christ. Be subject to one another because you reverence Christ.

PAUL'S general appeal finishes with an exhortation to his converts to live like wise men. The times in which they are living are evil; they must rescue as much time as they can from the evil uses of the world.

He goes on to draw a contrast between a pagan gathering and a Christian gathering. The pagan gathering is apt to be a debauch. It is significant that we still use the word *symposium* for a discussion of a subject by a number of people; the Greek word *sumposion* literally means a drinking-party. Once A. C. Welch was preaching on this text: "Be filled with the Spirit." He began with one sudden sentence: "You've got to fill a man with something." The heathen found his happiness in filling himself with wine and with worldly pleasures; the Christian found his happiness in being filled with the Spirit.

From this passage we can gather certain facts about the Christian gatherings in the early days.

(i) The early Church was a *singing Church*. Its characteristic was psalms and hymns and spiritual songs; it had a happiness which made men sing.

(ii) The early Church was a *thankful Church*. The instinct was to give thanks for all things and in all places and at all times. Chrysostom, great preacher of the Church of a later day, had the curious thought that a Christian could give thanks even for Hell, because Hell was a warning to keep him in the right way. The early Church was a thankful Church because its members were still dazzled with the wonder that God's love had stooped to save them; and it was a thankful Church because its members had such a consciousness that they were in the hands of God.

(iii) The early Church was a Church where men *honoured and respected each other*. Paul says that the reason for this mutual honour and respect was that they reverenced Christ. They saw each other not in the light of their professions or social standing but in the light of Christ; and therefore they saw the dignity of every man.

THE PRECIOUS BOND

Ephesians 5: 22–33

Wives, be subject to your husbands as to the Lord; for the husband is the head of the wife, even as Christ is the head of the Church, though there is this great difference, that Christ is the Saviour of the whole body. But, even allowing for this difference, even as the Church is subject to Christ, so wives must be subject to their husbands in everything. Husbands, love your wives, even as Christ loved the Church and gave himself for the Church, that by the washing of water he might purify her and consecrate her as she made confession of her faith, that he might make the Church to stand in his presence in all her glory, without any spot which soils, or any wrinkle which disfigures, or any such imperfection, but that she might be consecrated and blameless. So ought husbands to love their wives, to love them as they love their own bodies. He who loves his wife really loves himself. For no one ever hated his own flesh; rather he nourishes it and cherishes it. So Christ loves the Church because we are parts of his body. For this cause a man will leave his father and his mother and will cleave to his wife, and the two will become one flesh. This is a symbol which is very great—I mean when it is seen as a symbol of the relationship between Christ and the Church. However that may be, let each and every one of you love his wife as he loves himself, and let the wife reverence her husband.

No one reading this passage in the twentieth century can fully realize how great it is. Throughout the years the Christian view of marriage has come to be widely accepted. It still is recognised as the ideal by the majority even in these permissive days. Even where practice has fallen short of that ideal, it has always been in the minds and hearts of men who live in a Christian situation. Marriage is regarded as the perfect union of body, mind and spirit between a man and a woman. But things were very different when Paul wrote. In this passage Paul is setting forth an ideal which shone with a radiant purity in an immoral world.

Let us look briefly at the situation against which Paul wrote this passage.

The Jews had a low view of women. In his morning prayer there was a sentence in which a Jewish man gave thanks that God had not made him "a Gentile, a slave or a woman." In Jewish law a woman was not a person, but a thing. She had no legal rights whatsoever; she was absolutely her husband's possession to do with as he willed.

In theory the Jew had the highest ideal of marriage. The Rabbis had their sayings. "Every Jew must surrender his life rather than commit idolatry, murder or adultery." "The very altar sheds tears when a man divorces the wife of his youth." But the fact was that by Paul's day, divorce had become tragically easy.

The law of divorce is summarized in *Deuteronomy* 24: 1. "When a man takes a wife and marries her, if then she finds no favour in his eyes because he has found some indecency in her, he writes her a bill of divorce and puts it in her hand and sends her out of his house." Obviously everything turns on the interpretation of *some indecency*. The stricter Rabbis, headed by the famous Shammai, held that the phrase meant adultery and adultery alone, and declared that even if a wife was as mischievous as Jezebel a husband might not divorce her except for adultery. The more liberal Rabbis, headed by the equally famous Hillel, interpreted the phrase in the widest possible way. They said that it meant that a man might divorce his wife if she spoiled his dinner by putting too much salt in his food, if she walked in public with her head uncovered, if she talked with men in the streets, if she spoke disrespectfully of her husband's parents in her husband's hearing, if she was a brawling woman, if she was troublesome or quarrelsome. A certain Rabbi Akiba interpreted the phrase *if she finds no favour in his eyes* to mean that a husband might divorce his wife if he found a woman whom he considered more attractive. It is easy to see which school of thought would predominate.

Two facts in Jewish law made the matter worse. First, the wife had no rights of divorce at all, unless her husband became a leper or an apostate or engaged in a disgusting trade. Broadly speaking, a husband, under Jewish law, could divorce his wife for any cause; a wife could divorce her husband for no cause. Second, the process of divorce was disastrously easy. The Mosaic law said that a man who wished a divorce had to hand his wife a bill of divorcement which said, "Let this be from me thy writ of divorce and letter of dismissal and deed of liberation, that thou mayest marry whatsoever man thou wilt." All a man had to do was to hand that bill of divorcement, correctly written out by a Rabbi, to his wife in the presence of two witnesses and the divorce was complete. The only other condition was that the woman's dowry must be returned.

At the time of Christ's coming the marriage bond was in peril even among the Jews, so much so that the very institution of marriage was threatened since Jewish girls were refusing to marry because their position as wife was so uncertain.

THE PRECIOUS BOND

Ephesians 5: 22–33 *(continued)*

THE situation was worse in the Greek world. Prostitution was an essential part of Greek life. Demosthenes had laid it down as the accepted rule of life: "We have courtesans for the sake of pleasure; we have concubines for the sake of daily co-habitation; we have wives for the purpose of having children legitimately and of having a faithful guardian for all our household affairs." The woman of the respectable classes in Greece led a completely secluded life. She took no part in public life; she never appeared on the streets alone; she never even appeared at meals or at social occasions; she had her own apartments and none but her husband might enter into them. It was the aim that, as Xenophon had it, "she might see as little as possible, hear as little as possible and ask as little as possible."

The Greek respectable woman was brought up in such a way that companionship and fellowship in marriage was im-possible. Socrates said: "Is there anyone to whom you entrust more serious matters than to your wife—and is there anyone to whom you talk less?" Verus was the imperial colleague of the great Marcus Aurelius. He was blamed by his wife for associating with other women, and his answer was that she must remember that the name of wife was a title of dignity but not of pleasure. The Greek expected his wife to run his home, to care for his legitimate children, but he found his pleasure and his companionship elsewhere.

To make matters worse, there was no legal procedure of divorce in Greece. As someone has put it, divorce was by nothing else than caprice. The one security that the wife had was that her dowry must be returned. Home and family life were near to being extinct and fidelity was completely non-existent.

THE PRECIOUS BOND

Ephesians 5: 22–33 *(continued)*

IN Rome the matter was still worse; its degeneracy was tragic. For the first five hundred years of the Roman Republic there had been not one single case of divorce. The first recorded divorce was that of Spurius Carvilius Ruga in 234 B.C. But at the time of Paul, Roman family life was wrecked. Seneca writes that women were married to be divorced and divorced to be married. In Rome the Romans did not commonly date their years by numbers; they called them by the names of the consuls; Seneca says that women dated the years by the names of their husbands. Martial tells of a woman who had had ten husbands; Juvenal tells of one who had had eight husbands in five years; Jerome declares it to be true that in Rome there was a woman who was married to her twenty-third husband and she herself was his twenty-first wife. We find a Roman Emperor Augustus demanding that her husband should divorce the lady Livia when she was with child that he might himself marry her. We find even Cicero, in his old age, putting away his wife Terentia that he might marry a young heiress, whose trustee he was, that he might enter into her estate in order to pay his debts.

That is not to say that there was no such thing as fidelity. Suetonius tells of a Roman lady called Mallonia who committed suicide rather than submit to the favours of Tiberius the Emperor. But it is not too much to say that the whole atmosphere was adulterous. The marriage bond was on the way to complete breakdown.

It is against this background that Paul writes. When he wrote this lovely passage he was not stating the view that every man held. He was calling men and women to a new purity and a new fellowship in the married life. It is impossible to exaggerate the cleansing effect that Christianity had on home life in the ancient world and the benefits it brought to women.

THE GROWTH OF PAUL'S THOUGHT

Ephesians 5: 22–33 *(continued)*

IN this passage we find Paul's real thought on marriage. There are things which Paul wrote about marriage which puzzle us and may make us wish that he had never written them. The unfortunate thing is that it is these things which are so often quoted as Paul's view of marriage.

One of the strangest chapters is 1 *Corinthians* 7. He is talking about marriage and about the relationships between men and women. The blunt truth is that Paul's teaching is that marriage is permissible merely in order to avoid something worse. "Because of the temptation to immorality," he writes, "each man should have his own wife and each woman her own husband" (1 *Corinthians* 7: 2). He allows that a widow may marry again but it would be better if she remained single (1 *Corinthians* 7: 39, 40). He would prefer the unmarried and the widows not to marry. "But if they cannot exercise self-control, they should marry; for it is better to marry than to be aflame with passion" (1 *Corinthians* 7: 9).

There was a reason why Paul wrote like that. It was because he hourly expected the Second Coming of Jesus. It was therefore his conviction that no one should undertake any earthly ties whatsoever, but that all should concentrate on using the short time which remained in preparing for the coming of their Lord. "The unmarried man is anxious about the affairs of the Lord, how to please the Lord; but the married man is anxious about worldly affairs, how to please his wife" (1 *Corinthians* 7: 32, 33).

Between 1 *Corinthians* and *Ephesians* there is a space of perhaps nine years. In these nine years Paul had realized that the Second Coming was not to be so soon as he had thought, that in fact he and his people were living, not in a temporary situation, but in a more or less permanent situation. And it is in *Ephesians* that we find Paul's true teaching on marriage, that Christian marriage is the most precious relationship in life, whose only parallel is the relationship between Christ and the Church.

It is just possible that the *Corinthians* passage was coloured by Paul's personal experience. It would seem that in his days as a zealous Jew, he was a member of the Sanhedrin. When he is telling of his conduct towards the Christians, he says: "I cast my vote against them" (*Acts* 26: 10). It would also seem that one of the qualifications for membership of the Sanhedrin was marriage, and that therefore Paul must have been a married man. He never mentions his wife. Why? It may well be that it was because she turned against him when he became a Christian. It may be that when he wrote 1 *Corinthians* Paul was speaking out of a situation in which, not only did he expect the immediate coming of Christ, but in which he had also found his own marriage one of his greatest problems and sorest heartbreaks; so that he saw marriage as a handicap for the Christian.

THE BASIS OF LOVE

Ephesians 5: 22–33 *(continued)*

SOMETIMES the emphasis of this passage is entirely misplaced; and it is read as if its essence was the subordination of wife to husband. The single phrase, "The husband is the head of the wife," is quoted in isolation. But the basis of the passage is not control; it is love. Paul says certain things about the love that a husband must bear his wife.

(i) It must be a *sacrificial* love. He must love her as Christ loved the Church and gave himself for the Church. It must never be a selfish love. Christ loved the Church, not that the Church might do things for him, but that he might do things for the Church. Chrysostom has a wonderful expansion of this passage: "Hast thou seen the measure of obedience? Hear also the measure of love. Wouldst thou that thy wife shouldst obey thee as the Church doth Christ? Have care thyself for her as Christ for the Church. And if it be needful that thou shouldst give thy life for her, or be cut to pieces a thousand times, or endure anything whatever, refuse it not. . . . He brought the Church to his feet by his great care, not by threats nor fear nor any such thing; so do thou conduct thyself towards thy wife."

The husband is head of the wife—true, Paul said that; but he also said that the husband must love the wife as Christ loved the Church, with a love which never exercises a tyranny of control but which is ready to make any sacrifice for her good.

(ii) It must be a *purifying* love. Christ cleansed and consecrated the Church by the washing of water on the day when each member of the Church took his confession of faith. It may well be that Paul has in mind a Greek custom. One of the Greek marriage customs was that before the bride was taken to her marriage she was bathed in the water of a stream sacred to some god or goddess. In Athens, for instance, the bride was bathed in the waters of the Callirhoe, which was sacred to the goddess Athene. It is of baptism that Paul is thinking. By the washing of baptism and by the confession of faith, Christ sought to make for himself a Church, cleansed and consecrated, until there was neither soiling spot nor disfiguring wrinkle upon it. Any love which drags a person down is false. Any love which coarsens instead of refining the character, which necessitates deceit, which weakens the moral fibre, is not love. Real love is the great purifier of life.

(iii) It must be a *caring* love. A man must love his wife as he loves his own body. Real love loves not to extract service, nor to ensure that its own physical comfort is attended to, it cherishes the one it loves. There is something far wrong when a man regards his wife, consciously or unconsciously, as simply the one who cooks his meals and washes his clothes and cleans his house and trains his children.

(iv) It is an *unbreakable* love. For the sake of this love a man leaves father and mother and cleaves to his wife. They become one flesh. He is as united to her as the members of the body are united to each other; and would no more think of separating from her than of tearing his own body apart. Here indeed was an ideal in an age when men and women changed partners with as little thought as they changed clothes.

(v) The whole relationship is *in the Lord*. In the Christian home Jesus is an ever-remembered, though an unseen, guest. In Christian marriage there are not two partners, but three—and the third is Christ.

CHILDREN AND PARENTS

Ephesians 6: 1–4

Children, obey your parents, as Christian children should. Honour your father and your mother—for this is the first commandment to which a promise is attached—that it may be well with you, and that you may live long on the earth. Fathers, do not move your children to anger, but bring them up in the discipline and the admonition of the Lord.

IF the Christian faith did much for women, it did even more for children. In Roman civilization contemporary with Paul there existed certain features which made life perilous for the child.

(i) There was the Roman *patria potestas,* the father's power. Under the *patria potestas* a Roman father had absolute power over his family. He could sell them as slaves, he could make them work in his fields even in chains, he could punish as he liked and could even inflict the death penalty. Further, the power of the Roman father extended over the child's whole life, so long as the father lived. A Roman son never came of age. Even when he was a grown man, even if he were a magistrate of the city, even if the state had crowned him with well-deserved honours, he remained within his father's absolute power. "The great mistake," writes Becker, "consisted in the Roman father considering the power which Nature imposes as a duty on the elders, of guiding and protecting a child during infancy, as extending over his freedom, involving his life and death, and continuing over his entire existence." It is true that the father's power was seldom carried to its limits, because public opinion would not have allowed it, but the fact remains that in the time of Paul the child was absolutely in his father's power.

(ii) There was the custom of child exposure. When a child was born, it was placed before its father's feet, and, if the father stooped and lifted the child, that meant that he acknowledged it and wished it to be kept. If he turned and walked away, it meant that he refused to acknowledge it and the child could quite literally be thrown out.

There is a letter whose date is 1 B.C. from a man called Hilarion to his wife Alis. He has gone to Alexandria and he writes home on domestic affairs:

"Hilarion to Alis his wife heartiest greetings, and to my dear Berous and Apollonarion. Know that we are still even now in Alexandria. Do not worry if when all others return I remain in Alexandria. I beg and beseech of you to take care of the little child, and, as soon as we receive wages, I will send them to you. If—good luck to you!—you have a child, if it is a boy, let it live; if it is a girl, throw it out. You told Aphrodisias to tell me: 'Do not forget me.' How can I forget you? I beg you therefore not to worry."

It is a strange letter, so full of affection and yet so callous towards the child who may be born.

A Roman baby always ran the risk of being repudiated and exposed. In the time of Paul that risk was even greater. We have seen how the marriage bond had collapsed and how men and women changed their partners with bewildering rapidity. Under such circumstances a child was a misfortune. So few children were born that the Roman government actually passed legislation that the amount of any legacy that a childless couple could receive was limited. Unwanted children were commonly left in the Roman forum. There they became the property of anyone who cared to pick them up. They were collected at nights by people who nourished them in order to sell them as slaves or to stock the brothels of Rome.

(iii) Ancient civilization was merciless to the sickly or deformed child. Seneca writes, "We slaughter a fierce ox; we strangle a mad dog; we plunge the knife into sickly cattle lest they taint the herd; children who are born weakly and deformed we drown." The child who was a weakling or imperfectly formed had little hope of survival.

It was against this situation that Paul wrote his advice to children and parents. If ever we are asked what good Christianity has done to the world, we need but point to the change effected in the status of women and of children.

CHILDREN AND PARENTS

Ephesians 6: 1–4 *(continued)*

PAUL lays on children that they should obey the commandment and honour their parents. He says this is the *first* commandment. He probably means that it was the first commandment which the Christian child was taught to memorize. The honour Paul demands is not the honour of mere lip service. The way to honour parents is to obey them, to respect them, and never to cause them pain.

Paul sees that there is another side to the question. He tells fathers that they must not provoke their children to wrath. Bengel, considering why this command is so definitely addressed to *fathers*, says that mothers have a kind of divine patience but "fathers are more liable to be carried away by wrath."

It is a strange thing that Paul repeats this injunction even more fully in *Colossians* 3: 21. "Fathers," he says, "do not provoke your children, *lest they become discouraged.*" Bengel says that the plague of youth is a "broken spirit," discouraged by continuous criticism and rebuke and too strict discipline. David Smith thinks that Paul wrote out of bitter personal experience. He writes: "There is here a quivering note of personal emotion, and it seems as though the heart of the aged captive had been reverting to the past and recalling the loveless years of his own childhood. Nurtured in the austere atmosphere of traditional orthodoxy, he had experienced scant tenderness and much severity, and had known that 'plague of youth, a broken spirit.' "

There are three ways in which we can do injustice to our children.

(i) We can forget that things do change and that the customs of one generation are not the customs of another. Elinor Mordaunt tells how once she stopped her little daughter from doing something by saying, "I was never allowed to do that when I was your age." And the child answered, "But you must remember, mother, that you were *then*, and I'm *now*."

(ii) We can exercise such a control that it is an insult to our upbringing of our children. To keep a child too long in leading-strings is simply to say that we do not trust him which is simply to say that we have no confidence in the way in which we have trained him. It is better to make the mistake of too much trust than of too much control.

(iii) We can forget the duty of encouragement. Luther's father was very strict, strict to the point of cruelty. Luther used to say: "Spare the rod and spoil the child—that is true; but beside the rod keep an apple to give him when he has done well." Benjamin West tells how he became a painter. One day his mother went out leaving him in charge of his little sister Sally. In his mother's absence he discovered some bottles of coloured ink and began to paint Sally's portrait. In doing so he made a considerable mess of things with ink blots all over. His mother came back. She saw the mess but said nothing. She picked up the piece of paper and saw the drawing. "Why," she said, "it's Sally!" and she stooped and kissed him. Ever after Benjamin West used to say: "My mother's kiss made me a painter." Encouragement did more than rebuke could ever do. Anna Buchan tells how her grandmother had a favourite phrase even when she was very old: "Never daunton youth."

As Paul sees it, children must honour their parents and parents must never discourage their children.

MASTERS AND SLAVES

Ephesians 6: 5–9

Slaves, obey your human masters with fear and trembling, in sincerity of heart, as you would Christ himself. Do not work only when you are being watched. Do not work only to satisfy men.

> But work as the slave of Christ, doing God's will heartily. Let your service be given with good-will, as to Christ and not to men. Be well assured that each of us, whether he is slave or free, will be rewarded by the Lord for whatever good we have done. And you masters, act in the same way towards your slaves. Have done with threats. For you well know that they and you have a Master in heaven, and with him there is no respect of persons.

WHEN Paul wrote to slaves in the Christian Church he must have been writing to a very large number.

It has been computed that in the Roman Empire there were 60,000,000 slaves. In Paul's day a kind of terrible idleness had fallen on the citizens of Rome. Rome was the mistress of the world, and therefore it was beneath the dignity of a Roman citizen to work. Practically all work was done by slaves. Even doctors and teachers, even the closest friends of the Emperors, their secretaries who dealt with letters and appeals and finance, were slaves.

Often there were bonds of the deepest loyalty and affection between master and slave. Pliny writes to a friend that he is deeply affected because some of his well-loved slaves have died. He has two consolations, although they are not enough to comfort his grief. "I have always very readily manumitted my slaves (for their death does not seem altogether untimely, if they have lived long enough to receive their freedom); the other, that I have allowed them to make a kind of will, which I observe as rigidly as if it were good in law." There the kindly master speaks.

But basically the life of the slave was grim and terrible. In law he was not a person but a *thing*. Aristotle lays it down that there can never be friendship between master and slave, for they have nothing in common; "for a slave is a living tool, just as a tool is an inanimate slave." Varro, writing on agriculture, divides agricultural instruments into three classes —the articulate, the inarticulate and the mute. The articulate comprises the slaves; the inarticulate the cattle; and the mute the vehicles. The slave is no better than a beast who happens to be able to talk. Cato gives advice to a man taking over a farm. He must go over it and throw out everything that is past its work; and old slaves too must be thrown out on the scrap heap to starve. When a slave is ill it is sheer extravagance to issue him with normal rations.

The law was quite clear. Gaius, the Roman lawyer, in the *Institutes* lays it down: "We may note that it is universally accepted that the master possesses the power of life and death over the slave." If the slave ran away, at best he was branded on the forehead with the letter F for *fugitivus,* which means runaway, at worst he was killed. The terror of the slave was that he was absolutely at the caprice of his master. Augustus crucified a slave because he killed a pet quail. Vedius Pollio flung a slave still living to the savage lampreys in his fish pond because he dropped and broke a crystal goblet. Juvenal tells of a Roman matron who ordered a slave to be killed for no other reason than that she lost her temper with him. When her husband protested, she said: "You call a slave a man, do you? He has done no wrong, you say? Be it so; it is my will and my command; let my will be the voucher for the deed." The slaves who were maids to their mistresses often had their hair torn out and their cheeks torn with their mistresses' nails. Juvenal tells of the master "who delights in the sound of a cruel flogging thinking it sweeter than any siren's song," or "who revels in clanking chains," or, "who summons a torturer and brands the slave because a couple of towels are lost." A Roman writer lays it down: "Whatever a master does to a slave, undeservedly, in anger, willingly, unwillingly, in forgetfulness, after careful thought, knowingly, unknowingly, is judgment, justice and law."

It is against this terrible background that Paul's advice to slaves has to be read.

MASTERS AND SLAVES

Ephesians 6: 5–9 *(continued)*

PAUL'S advice to slaves provides us with the gospel of the Christian workman.

(i) He does not tell them to rebel; he tells them to be Christian where they are. The great message of Christianity to every man is that it is where God has set us that we must live out the Christian life. The circumstances may be all against us, but that only makes the challenge greater. Christianity does not offer us escape from circumstances; it offers us conquest of circumstances.

(ii) He tells the slaves that work must not be done well only when the overseer's eye is on them; it must be done in the awareness that God's eye is on them. Every single piece of work the Christian produces must be good enough to show to God. The problem that the world has always faced and that it faces acutely today is basically not economic but religious. We will never make men good workmen by bettering conditions or heightening rewards. It is a Christian duty to see to these things; but in themselves they will never produce good work. Still less will we produce good work by increasing oversight and multiplying punishments. The secret of good workmanship is to do it for God.

Paul has a word for the master of men, too. He must remember that although he is master of men, he is still the servant of God. He too must remember that all he does is done in the sight of God. Above all he must remember that the day comes when he and those over whom he is set will stand before God; and then the ranks of the world will no longer be relevant.

The problem of work would be solved if men and masters alike would take their orders from God.

THE ARMOUR OF GOD

Ephesians 6: 10–20

> Finally, be strong in the Lord and in the power of his strength. Put on the armour of God, so that you may be able to stand against the devices of the devil. It is not with blood and flesh you have to wrestle, but against powers and against authorities, against

the world rulers of this darkness, against malicious spiritual forces in the heavenly places. Because of this you must take the armour of God that you may be able to stand against them in the evil day, and that you may be able to stand fast, after you have done all things which are your duty. Stand with truth as a belt about your waist. Put on righteousness as a breastplate. Have your feet shod with readiness to preach the gospel of peace. In all things take faith as a shield for with it you will be able to quench the flaming darts of the evil one. Put on the helmet of salvation. Take the sword of the Spirit, which is the word of God. Keep praying in the Spirit at every crisis with every kind of prayer and entreaty to God. To that end be sleepless in your persevering prayer for all God's consecrated people. Pray for me that I may be allowed to speak with open mouth, and boldly to make known the secret of the gospel, for which I am an envoy in a chain. Pray that I may have freedom to declare it, as I ought to speak.

As Paul takes leave of his people he thinks of the greatness of the struggle which lies before them. Undoubtedly life was much more terrifying for the ancient people than it is for us today. They believed implicitly in evil spirits, who filled the air and were determined to work men harm. The words which Paul uses, powers, authorities, world-rulers, are all names for different classes of these evil spirits. To him the whole universe was a battleground. The Christian had not only to contend with the attacks of men; he had to contend with the attacks of spiritual forces which were fighting against God. We may not take Paul's actual language literally; but our experience will tell us that there is an active power of evil in the world. Robert Louis Stevenson once said: "You know the Caledonian Railway Station in Edinburgh? One cold, east windy morning, I met Satan there." We do not know what actually befell Stevenson but we recognize the experience; we have all felt the force of that evil influence which seeks to make us sin.

Paul suddenly sees a picture ready-made. All this time he was chained by the wrist to a Roman soldier. Night and day a soldier was there to ensure that he would not escape. Paul was literally an envoy in a chain. Now he was the kind of man who could get alongside anyone; and beyond doubt he had talked often to the soldiers who were compelled to be so near him. As he writes, the soldier's armour suggests a picture to him. The Christian too has his armour; and part by part Paul takes the armour of the Roman soldier and translates it into Christian terms.

There is the belt of truth. It was the belt which girt in the soldier's tunic and from which his sword hung and which gave him freedom of movement. Others may guess and grope; the Christian moves freely and quickly because he knows the truth.

There is the breastplate of righteousness. When a man is clothed in righteousness he is impregnable. Words are no defence against accusations but a good life is. Once a man accused Plato of certain crimes. "Well then," said Plato, "we must live in such a way as to prove that his accusations are a lie." The only way to meet the accusations against Christianity is to show how good a Christian can be.

There are the sandals. Sandals were the sign of one equipped and ready to move. The sign of the Christian is that he is eager to be on the way to share the gospel with others who have not heard it.

There is the shield. The word Paul uses is not that for the comparatively small round shield; it is that for the great oblong shield which the heavily armed warrior wore. One of the most dangerous weapons in ancient warfare was the fiery dart. It was a dart tipped with tow dipped in pitch. The pitch-soaked tow was set alight and the dart was thrown. The great oblong shield was made of two sections of wood, glued together. When the shield was presented to the dart, the dart sank into the wood and the flame was put out. Faith can deal with the darts of temptation. With Paul, faith is always complete trust in Christ. When we walk close with Christ, we are safe from temptation.

There is salvation for a helmet. Salvation is not something which looks back only. The salvation which is in Christ gives us forgiveness for the sins of the past and strength to conquer sin in the days to come.

There is the sword; and the sword is the word of God. The word of God is at once our weapon of defence against sin and our weapon of attack against the sins of the world. Cromwell's Ironsides fought with a sword in one hand and a Bible in the other. We can never win God's battles without God's book.

Finally, Paul comes to the greatest weapon of all—and that is prayer. We note three things that he says about prayer. (*a*) It must be constant. Our tendency is so often to pray only in the great crises of life; but it is from daily prayer that the Christian will find daily strength. (*b*) It must be intense. Limp prayer never got a man anywhere. Prayer demands the concentration of every faculty upon God. (*c*) It must be unselfish. The Jews had a saying, "Let a man unite himself with the community in his prayers." I think that often our prayers are too much for ourselves and too little for others. We must learn to pray as much for others and with others as for ourselves.

Finally, Paul asks for the prayers of his friends for himself. And he asks not for comfort or for peace but that he may yet be allowed to proclaim God's secret, that his love is for all men. We do well to remember that ever Christian leader and every Christian preacher needs his people to uphold his hands in prayer.

THE FINAL BLESSING

Ephesians 6: 21–24

Tychicus, the beloved brother and faithful servant in the Lord, will provide you with all information, that you too may know how things are going with me, how I do. That is the very reason that I sent him to you, that you may know my affairs and that he may encourage your hearts.

Peace be to the brethren, and love with faith, from God the Father and from the Lord Jesus Christ. Grace be with all who love the Lord Jesus with a love which defies death.

As we have seen, the letter to the Ephesians was an encyclical letter and the bearer from church to church was Tychicus. Unlike most of his letters, *Ephesians* gives us no personal information about Paul, except that he was in prison; but Tychicus, as he went from church to church, would tell how Paul was faring and would convey a message of personal encouragement.

Paul finishes with a blessing—and in it all the great words come again. The peace which was a man's highest good, the faith which was complete resting in Christ, the grace which was the lovely free gift of God—these things Paul calls down from God upon his friends. Above all he prays for love that they may know the love of God, that they may love men as God loves them, and that they may love Jesus Christ with an undying love.

FURTHER READING

Galatians

E. D. Burton, *Galatians* (ICC; *G*)
G. S. Duncan, *The Epistle to the Galatians* (MC; *E*)
D. Guthrie, *Galatians* (NCB; *E*)
J. B. Lightfoot, *The Epistle to the Galatians* (MmC; *G*)

Ephesians

T. K. Abbott, *Ephesians and Colossians* (ICC; *G*)
J. Armitage Robinson, *St. Paul's Epistle to the Ephesians* (MmC; *G*)
E. F. Scott, *The Epistles to Colossians, Philemon and Ephesians* (MC; *E*)

Abbreviations

ICC : International Critical Commentary
MC : Moffatt Commentary
MmC : Macmillan Commentary
NCB : New Century Bible

E : English Text
G : Greek Text

THE DAILY STUDY BIBLE

Published in 17 Volumes